PRAISE FOR KAREN CASEY

"Karen Casey captures the experience, strength, and hope that are essential to maintaining healthy relationships with each other and with ourselves."

—WILLIAM C. MOYERS, author of *Broken*

"You just can't go wrong with Karen Casey."

—EARNIE LARSEN, author of *Stage II Recovery* and *From Anger to Forgiveness*

"Karen Casey's honesty about detachment as a lifelong process brings comfort and encouragement. Thanks, Karen, for writing this book and for a lifetime of dedicated service that has made this world a better place."

—MELODY BEATTIE, author of *Codependent No More*

"Veteran self-help author Casey's gentle advice is anchored in a strong spiritual commitment… [She] recommends quieting the mind by letting go of your ego and looking for the lesson in every experience and encounter, whether positive or negative. Casey's voice is thoughtful and accessible."

—*Publishers Weekly*

"*Codependence and the Power of Detachment* should be required reading for all who seek to create healthy, balanced relationships in their lives."

—CLAUDIA BLACK, PhD, author of *It Will Never Happen to Me*

"*Codependence and the Power of Detachment* is a remarkable book written in easy-to-understand language with great honesty."

—JERRY JAMPOLSKY, MD, founder of the International Center for Attitudinal Healing

"*Change Your Mind and Your Life* Will Follow tells the truth and tells it well. I recommend it."

—MARIANNE WILLIAMSON, author of *The Gift of Change: Spiritual Guidance for a Radically New Life*

"*All We Have Is All We Need* is a gem of a book! So much wisdom and peace in every paragraph and sentence. These inspirational, quotable thoughts constantly affirm the incredible fruits of simply shifting our perspective—through the uniquely human gift of choice."

—STEPHEN R. COVEY, author of *The 7 Habits of Highly Effective People*

"Once again Karen Casey helps us know the difference between an honest energy-draining crisis and a wrinkle in the sheet. Through her personal life encounters, Casey illustrates the wisdom gained when one follows her spirit. What a model for those who seek to find and listen to their inner voice. *Change Your Mind and Your Life Will Follow* offers clear and simple life instructions. A must-read book!"

—MARILYN J. MASON, PhD, author of *Igniting the Spirit at Work*

"The experience of hope, as Karen Casey so intelligently and gently explains, comes from success. However, most of us are not ready for huge, life-changing successes. But we can all succeed in small ways each day, if we know how to proceed. It is warm, wise, personal, and welcoming—an invaluable tool for spiritual growth that I highly recommend."

—HUGH PRATHER, author of *How to Live in the World and Still Be Happy, Standing on My Head,* and *Shining Through*

"This is an absolutely wonderful, magical, and deeply transforming book. It is a small book that can have a big impact. It inspires, guides, and challenges as it provides a practical design for living. No matter where I opened the book, I seemed always to be on the right page. A must-read for anyone who seeks the kind of livable truths that can lead to serenity and a sense of life as a spiritual adventure."

—TIAN DAYTON, PhD, author of *Trauma and Addiction, The Magic of Forgiveness,* and *Forgiving and Moving On*

The
Good
Stuff
from Growing Up in a Dysfunctional Family

The Good Stuff

from Growing Up in a Dysfunctional Family

How to Survive and Then Thrive

Karen Casey

Conari Press

First published in 2013 by Conari Press, an imprint of
Red Wheel/Weiser, LLC
With offices at:
665 Third Street, Suite 400
San Francisco, CA 94107
www.redwheelweiser.com

Library of Congress Cataloging-in-Publication Data
Casey, Karen.
  The good stuff from growing up in dysfunctional families : how to survive and
then thrive / Karen Casey.
     pages cm
  Summary: "Is there a silver lining to growing up in a dysfunctional family?
Bestselling recovery author Karen Casey looks at stories of people who grew up
in dysfunctional families and "the good stuff" that can come from the experience.
"Throughout my many decades in recovery rooms I have interacted with thousands of women and men whose journeys reveal, in detail, the harrowing history
of dysfunction that has troubled their lives," says Casey. "But what is also apparent in their stories is their eventual and quite triumphant survival, often against
extreme odds." Casey interviewed more than 24 survivors of families rife with
dysfunction; survivors who willingly shared their stories and came to realize they
had, surprisingly, thrived as the result of their often harrowing experiences. In
The Good Stuff from Growing Up in a Dysfunctional Family, Casey shares the
stories and the skills these survivors developed to live more creative and fulfilling
lives"—Provided by publisher.
  ISBN 978-1-57324-596-8 (pbk.)
  1. Adult children of dysfunctional families—Psychology. 2. Dysfunctional
families—Psychological aspects. 3. Perseveration (Psychology) 4. Resilience
(Personality trait) 5. Self-esteem. I. Title.

  RC455.4.F3.C37 2013
  616.89—dc23

                          2013026798

Cover design by Jim Warner
Interior by Maureen Forys, Happenstance Type-O-Rama
Typeset in Bembo and Universe

Printed in the United States of America
MAL

10 9 8 7 6 5 4 3 2 1

CONTENTS

INTRODUCTION

Over the course of my many decades in recovery rooms, I've interacted with thousands of women and men whose journeys reveal, in detail, the harrowing history of dysfunction that has troubled their lives. Listening to their accounts, and being witness to these painful and difficult struggles, I've often been amazed by the speakers themselves—at their openness, resilience, sense of humor, courage, and most of all their eventual and quite triumphant survival, often against extreme odds. For many years I've been fascinated by the idea that when we grow up in a dysfunctional family, we have access to a host of benefits we otherwise might not be privy to. This is rarely spoken of or written about, I think partly because it seems strange for us to think of abuse and neglect offering any kind of potential value in our lives. But those of us who have grown up in dysfunctional families know that this upbringing has served us with special gifts, and that each challenge comes with new opportunities. The very dysfunction these people lived through taught them— sometimes in reacting against it, sometimes in discovering the whys and wherefores of it—survival skills for life beyond dysfunction. They found that there are, in fact, many silver linings, maybe even nuggets of gold.

In writing this book, I set out with this assignment, one I'm certain I have been "called" to do: to interview more than two dozen men and women, to listen deeply to their stories and tease out their unique traits and perspectives. Did you know that to interview means simply "to see each other?" I wanted to see these people clearly, and to share with you a detailed description of twelve positive characteristics that are ready to be born in you and then become honed, just as they were in the people from these dysfunctional families.

These twelve traits open the door to successful living. The stories I have selected from among the many I heard clearly demonstrate what is really possible when a person not only rises to the occasion to change and grow, but exceeds all expectations in a family that could have doomed him or her to failure.

As I observed these journeys, those I saw up close and those, too, from afar, I saw that they were all astounding in one way or another, which might be said, really, about the path each of us takes. I was afforded many *aha!* moments as I noted the specific tools that these people mastered and the positive qualities that they developed along the way. In my conversations, I came to truly appreciate the gifts that we are given, even in those very circumstances that look so bleak to those who watch from outside the family circle.

The act of listening is a gift we can always offer another soul sharing our path. My role with those I interviewed was so intimate, really, as they revealed who they were, what happened, and who they are now. In every instance, what had been a downward spiraling life became an example of miraculous survival, offering proof to others that nothing has to defeat us. Through this process, I grew in my appreciation of the importance of both storytelling and being a witness to the story. The exchange moves us, connects us, allowing us to see our own lives with greater clarity, understanding, and openness. We are moved, too, to make some of the changes we see in the stories of others.

We often read and hear the "poor me" stories of those who are certain they were given a bum ride in this life. All we have to do is turn on daytime television, Dr. Phil, or reality shows for the anecdotes to support this assessment. But I have come to believe, and believe unequivocally, that we *choose* the ride we are on, one experience after another. We are not victims. We are volunteers. And that knowledge has made all the difference in the world to me. Suffice it to say that many will always live in the world of "poor me." That's where they feel most at ease. Without a doubt, they selected this journey, whether they realize it or not, and our observation of their journey surely informs the rest of us in a most interesting way, if we are open to the education.

Generally speaking, I think, those sad individuals hope to find others who will commiserate—who will say, "Of course you have every good reason to feel bad. You didn't deserve this set of experiences." And they often *do* find someone who will commiserate. Misery loves company. Uncomfortably, I admit I used to be that person. Perhaps it was a necessary part of my journey then. But no more. I think we learn from the mistakes as well as the wisdom of others; I have learned from mine along with all of those individuals I interviewed. What I hope to impart in this book is some of both, with an emphasis on the wisdom.

In this book, you will hear stories of successful survival, including my own, and you will be offered some specific tools for changing your own stories and cultivating your own gifts, if that's your desire. It was these stories of survival I wanted to tell, stories rife with rich rewards, stories that reveal phenomenal growth, stories that stand as examples to others still trapped in dysfunctional systems. It's my hope that this book will serve as a much-needed resource of hope when the reader doubts his or her capacity to survive within a family that seems destined to create doom and destruction at every turn.

My family was dysfunctional, though I didn't know to call it that when I was growing up. I simply knew it didn't feel good to be home. I often felt alone even in the midst of family gatherings. Virginia Satir, a psychotherapist who wrote many books and helped millions try to make sense of their family of origin, wrote that in the early 70s, 98 percent of all families were dysfunctional. I can still remember hearing that percentage and reading her book, *Self Esteem*. That percentage both astounded me and offered me some relief. Maybe my family wasn't so different from other families, after all. I had no idea then that my own life was about to turn a corner. But it did. My search was on for a better sense of self. It was a long search, of course, and it took me down many dark alleys, but I did find the light and I am here to tell you about it.

I think that's the assignment for all of us who have a story (and we all have a story)—*to share*. That's why your journey has intersected with mine, as we meet here in these pages. Satir crossed my path through the words of a book, and I took notice. That's what I hope this book does for you. I hope it helps you to take notice of your life, what it was, what it is now, and with some consideration what it can become. I'm certain that the many characteristics and tools that I'll share throughout this book will make your life more manageable and adaptable to the circumstances you face daily.

It's my desire that you will read the book with hope ignited that your own life can be bettered, just as the lives of all of these people were improved because they didn't run, they didn't give up, and they didn't feel shortchanged, at least not for long. They simply lived and looked for the gold hidden within the rubble of their family experiences. No family dynamic, lingering though it may be, has to overwhelm us unendingly. This I promise you. The gold is always there, I promise you.

1

Nourishing Resilience

Someone was hurt before you, wronged before you, hungry before you, frightened before you, beaten before you, humiliated before you, raped before you . . . yet, someone survived . . . You can do anything you choose to do.

Maya Angelou

In the face of humiliation, rage, degradation, fear of defeat, or simply indefinable fear, being resilient weaves the fabric of eventual success. Rebounding and recovering from the personal insults that life hands us contributes to our eventual growth. Whether these hard times are large or small, overt or covert, physical, mental, or emotional, whether they come from our family of origin, our workplace, or even our circle of friends, these very experiences that could stunt our development instead strengthen it, if we are resilient.

Resilience is standing tall rather than hanging our heads and shuffling away when the invitation to give up beckons. Resilience is saying, "Yes I can," in the presence of those who doubt us. Resilience means never succumbing to the forces of defeat that may be all around us.

Few of us graciously accept the insults that so commonly become a natural part of living. That's to be expected, perhaps. But what we manage to tolerate successfully, we will thrive from in time. That's my experience, anyway. And that's the experience I think we can all cultivate. That's the experience I hope to help you develop using the suggestions I offer in this book.

Ever since publishing my first book, *Each Day a New Beginning,* in 1982, I have become convinced that my calling, so to speak, is to serve as your teacher in any way that I can. By that I mean that I am called to share with you all that I have gathered from others over the years. Through my sharing, I get the added pleasure of *relearning* all that I offer you.

I chose to begin this book with a discussion of resilience because I think it is the kernel that lives at the center of all the positive characteristics we develop when we grow up in families that struggle to be functional. There are countless other strengths that will get our focus in due course, and throughout this book we will look at how resilience informs all of the experiences we face as we try to make sense of the dysfunctional family system.

Resilience means believing there is a path that has been charted for you and staying on it even when you stumble.

Resilience serves as a backdrop for lives that move forward rather than succumbing to the pain and the downdraft of the unenlightened family of origin. I say unenlightened because my research for this book has convinced me that families, for the most part, did the best they could; their best was simply seldom good enough because it wasn't well informed. And since that was the case, I think it's fair to say it took a herculean effort by the many individuals who have crossed my path to thrive, regardless of their circumstances.

One of the many people I interviewed, whose effort to survive was herculean, for sure, comes instantly to mind. His name has been changed to protect his anonymity. I'll call him William. William grew up in a family extremely short on compassionate attention and very long on his mother's withering criticism, coupled with extended periods of deadly silence. His mother, though not officially diagnosed, was mentally ill. And his father was a withdrawn, silent man, uninvolved and completely distant from his wife and two children. His work consumed him, perhaps as an escape, but nonetheless he was not available for emotional support, guidance, or any expression of love.

The family simply didn't function as a unit, but rather like four separate souls sharing the same address. They didn't create a home. Their interactions were few, with the exception of excessive outbursts of criticism from Mom, followed by the nearly immediate disappearance of Dad. My own family resembled William's in some regard. Although there was no mental illness, there was evidence of extreme emotional pain and measurable rage. The punishing silences, coupled with the frequent outbursts by my dad, made the hours at home uncertain, uncomfortable, and unenjoyable.

Children like William, and myself too, sought support and a sense of well-being from others. In William's case, he began to excel in school, reading all the books he could lay his hands on and seeking the approval of his instructors for evidence that he mattered, that he was worthy. William soon excelled at learning how to hide his own feelings of inadequacy.

Resilience means being a willing example for others that you can make lemonade even when the lemons come in bushels.

I, on the other hand, rebelled. I met rage with rage. However, I also sought a creative outlet: I began writing stories of happy families and pretending that I was a member of those families. It was a way to lessen the emotional blows, and it proved to prepare me for a later time in my life. The present time, in fact.

That's one of the hallmarks of resilience. We grow into the person we are (knowingly or unknowingly) cultivated to become by our family of origin. It doesn't matter, actually, how we get there. It's the becoming that's important. Just as Angelou said in the quote that begins this chapter, the history of pain that pushes us forward needn't be our focus. It's that we pushed forward. We survived. And we agreed to make the journey.

I asked a number of my interviewees what resilience meant to them. I got myriad answers, but the crux was the same. Most simply, resilience meant not giving up. But beyond that, it meant making the best of whatever the situation was. It meant searching for the "pony in the pile of hay."

To Charlie, it meant not giving up on his dream of being an aviator, even in the face of his father's constant criticism. Being told he'd never succeed in fact pushed him to prove otherwise. In the end, he not only flew professionally for a major airline, but has built two full-scale airplanes since retiring.

He was certainly wounded by the criticism heaped on him as a youngster and even into adulthood. But his dream was never thwarted. The dream was bigger than the criticism. Not everyone is able to rise above without help, however, and that's the reason for a book like this: to help those who are still struggling to put the past to bed by revealing true stories of others who trudged a similar path—people who found a way to move forward with a certainty that was unthinkable in their youth.

....

Resilience means not letting failure or criticism deter you from the willingness to try again. To move forward, regardless.

....

I found this to be the case for a number of the interviewees, in fact. For Judith, her dad was the "bully." The criticism was not only aimed at her, but also at her mother and her younger brother. Judith developed a hard exterior much like her dad's. However, she was as afraid as he was. Eventually she came to appreciate the fear that ruled his life. She also observed how his behavior created fear in the lives of her mother and younger brother. The tension in their home was palpable, she said, and nothing seemed to lessen it. A drink or two might relax her dad, but the clenched hands and raised voice were always just a breath or a moment away.

Fortunately for Judith, she knew she wanted to teach, she knew she wanted to write, she knew she wanted to help others. The life experiences with a rageful dad and a dispirited mother that might have drowned her actually served as a lifeboat for bringing her story of survival to others. Even though I will share much more about Judith later, let me assure you that she was a "good student" of human behavior and watching her parents taught her well about who to be and who not to be. For now let me simply say that she didn't maintain her hard exterior forever. Even though her father was never ever able to shed his, she came to understand and to develop compassion for what had initiated his attitude and took that information and used it in her own life so that she didn't have to repeat his pattern.

We are imprinted by the experiences we have as youngsters in our family of origin. Some research even suggests that we are imprinted while still in the womb. Some pregnant mothers play Beethoven or fill the house with fragrant flowers and the sounds of quiet rain on the roof or music meditations—who's to say those techniques don't have a beneficial effect?

I too was imprinted in the womb, but not with the soft sounds of a bubbling brook. I didn't know what exactly I had been imprinted with until well into my adult years. Let me share the backstory. From childhood on, I suffered the dread of impending doom in the form of a certainty that I was soon to be rejected, by whomever, for whatever reason. This fear haunted me as a young girl among my girlfriends and as a teenager trying desperately to attract and keep a boyfriend. Though my exterior looked hard, just like my dad's had looked, my interior was a constant jumble of nerves. My unease wherever I was influenced every interaction I had.

Resilience is letting the past be past rather than allowing it to control the present or forecast the future.

Of course I carried this uncertainty into every relationship. I watched my partners like a hawk, certain they were soon to dump me. And dump me they did, of course. My terror about abandonment escalated. It brought tension into a marriage that was troubled by alcohol from the start. My tension, and his too, coupled with our alcoholism, made manifest my worst fear. He abandoned me for another woman.

The result was that his action propelled me deeper into my alcoholism, which was fortunately followed by eventual sobriety. It was in early sobriety that I sought the help of a counselor because my fears around abandonment continued to negatively impact my behavior in every romantic relationship, and with every friend. The counselor's nearly first words were, "You were abandoned in the womb." What allowed her to intuit this I'll never know, but I didn't doubt, even for a moment, that she was right. However, what to do with this information provided my next stumbling block.

Not coincidentally, I was enrolled in a class on the dynamics of the family of origin at the same time. The two experiences, in combination, changed my life in a profound way. The teacher of the family of origin class assigned each one of us to talk to our families, particularly our parents, about their life experiences. The purpose was to see how our experiences mirrored theirs, or perhaps were a reaction to theirs in some significant way. I made the call to my parents, explaining that I wanted to interview them. The silence on the other end of the line was deafening, but they agreed to my request. I went home to talk to them a couple of weeks later. And my life made a right turn!

Resilience is a decision before it's anything else. And then it's a commitment to execute the plan.

I sat with my mother first, bless her heart. For sure neither of them wanted to be interrogated, but she did the motherly thing and agreed to go first. "Tell me about your life, Mom?" Almost immediately, the tears began to flow and then turned into sobs. "I never felt like a good wife, a good mother, and I didn't want you when I was pregnant with you." Bingo. My counselor had nailed it. My life began to make sense. The abandonment issue that had plagued me my entire life *was born in the womb*. Having this confirmed at age thirty-eight shed light on my journey, a light that has never been dimmed.

When I spoke to my dad, he shared openly the fear he had lived with his entire life, a fear that was shrouded in rage. At the time, it was a new concept for me to see rage as the cover-up for fear, but it made perfect sense. Rage kept people "in their place" and away from the interior spaces of his being. What an eye-opener my trip home was. My own hard exterior began to develop cracks, and my incessant certainty that every relationship in my life was on a trajectory of inevitable rejection began to ease.

With my changed perception about how life was unfolding, I became more willing to trust the process of daily life and to embrace each experience as the next perfect one. This allowed me to truly feel resilient and undaunted. I no longer waited for the bottom to fall out of my world. I no longer waited for everyone else to define my happiness. Being resilient makes it viable to stand tall rather than be knocked down. We can make a decision to stand, resilient, as every wave of experience hits us.

Resilience wears many coats. One of the more brilliant ones is worn by Allison, a fascinating interviewee. She was the first in her very large family to seek help for her addiction. Perhaps I shouldn't say she sought the help. She was institutionalized first, and an insightful counselor could see that her problem wasn't as simple as extreme incorrigibility but rather alcoholism. The acting out, which included running away and frequent fights in bars, was her cry for help—a cry neither she nor her family recognized initially.

Allison's story is long and complicated and I will cover many parts of it throughout this book, but right now I want to highlight her resilience. She has a truckload of it. She was the middle child in a family of eight children. It was easy to get overlooked in a family of that size, particularly when it was troubled by alcoholism too. Her acting out was probably a way of seeking attention, but it was also the direct result of drinking uncontrollably and doing drugs. For sure it won her attention, but not the kind she really wanted.

Following treatment for the mental problems and the alcoholism, she married. Her life seemed to settle for a time, but her decision to have children meant giving up the medication that stabilized her. Back into the hospital she went, but this time it didn't feel like prison. She found her equilibrium again. She kept going back every time there was a setback. It was as though her lesson in life was to rebound and show the rest of us what resilience looked like.

Resilience is a trait that can be honed by all but is avoided by many because of fear of failure.

Her struggles were far from over, however, and when her children were small, she was diagnosed with bone cancer. Her pelvic bone was removed and she lived in a body cast, for the most part immobile, for an entire year. How she managed that test of acceptance was amazing to everyone who knew her. And if the result of this trial was the freedom to walk again once the year was over, one might understand how she managed to live it. But that outcome was not to be—never again would Allison walk unaided.

She is a testament to resilience, however. She lives with joy and a sense of humor about the insanity of life. Her life was the embodiment of dysfunction, starting with the family she was born into and moving into her own diseased body. But nothing has kept her down. She lives her life to the fullest and helps others live theirs too. She did not transfer the dysfunction she was imprinted with in her family of origin to her own family. She broke the pattern. She blocked the trail of alcoholism.

For sure it could be said that every person I spoke to about survival in a family that seemed destined to defeat them actually gained strength from the experience. As is so commonly said, what doesn't kill you makes you stronger. Perhaps no one reflected this more than Dawn. Dawn is an Oneida Indian from Wisconsin. I met her in the rooms of Alcoholics Anonymous. I had no idea when I met her that we would travel this same path for nearly three decades, a path we still travel, in fact. Dawn is an amazing woman, one of sixteen kids, one of only seven still alive. Alcoholism has taken the lives of all the rest of them.

There is nothing about Dawn's upbringing that would have suggested she'd be one of the survivors. But survive she has, and thrive she does in her own way. It would be a vast understatement to say that her family was dysfunctional. Both parents were dead from alcoholism in their early 50s. Her father shot himself because he couldn't stop drinking. Her mother died of liver disease. All sixteen children were placed in foster care and Dawn and her younger sisters were molested again and again. The authorities never stepped in.

Dawn has carried the guilt over not being able to protect her younger sisters all of her life. She began to drink and gamble and run away as a way of coping at thirteen, and her path was grooved by the time she was sixteen. Amazingly, she proved to be a good employee for many years, in spite of her alcoholism and absenteeism. The past eventually caught up with her, however, and she was brutally beaten by a cop using a billy club while in a drunk tank. Many brain surgeries were not able to repair the damage that was inflicted on her. Her speech continues to be affected, as is her handwriting.

Resilience is getting up again and again when one falls.

Dawn has rebounded from unbelievable odds. She now has Parkinson's disease, along with the brain damage. Her gait is compromised. The seizures from epilepsy hit at the most unexpected times. Fortunately she receives disability and food stamps and is able to work part time, which gets her out of the house and around people two or three hours a day. A friend picks her up for AA meetings and an ex-husband makes sure she gets to family functions.

In spite of all the challenges, Dawn does not complain. She feels lucky to be alive and to have friends and family who continue to love her even though she put them through hell. She is determined to hold her head high and continue to face the world with dignity. She sees the bright side of life, even though her own life has been mostly dark. She helps others see the humor in the unexpected occurrences of daily life. She laughs heartily at herself and helps others to do likewise. She is the epitome of resilience.

When I consider all of the people I spoke to for this book, I'd have to say Dawn ranks at the top of the resilience list. Nothing could destroy her, no matter how dire—sexual abuse, rape, being beaten by cops, being jailed, going through detox and treatment more than two dozen times. Nothing kept her from continuing to put one foot in front of the other. And now at sixty she models to others that no matter how hard life is, taking it one day at a time makes it tolerable. Survivable. Even enjoyable.

Before moving on, let me reiterate some of the ideas outlined here for easy reference and as a practical outline for changing your behavior. To be resilient means being willing to try again, even when the odds don't look good.

It means not letting failure deter you from the willingness to keep trying—to move forward regardless.

It means believing there is a path that has been charted for you and staying on it even when you stumble.

It means being a willing example for others that you can make lemonade even when the lemons come in bushels.

Resilience is a trait that can be honed by all but is avoided by many because of fear of failure. (I'm reminded of the story about Thomas Edison and his perfection of the light bulb. He made more than five thousand attempts before he succeeded in getting one that continued to burn, and he was convinced that every one of the failures was serving the purpose of getting him closer to his goal.)

There is nothing magical about resilience. It's a decision before it's anything else. And then it's a commitment to execute the plan. Every story I shared in this chapter, brief though they were, provided an example of how really simple it is to demonstrate resilience.

It's getting up again and again when one falls.

It's letting the past be past rather than allowing it to control the present or forecast the future.

Dawn, for example, might well have given up dozens of times, but quitting wasn't in her vocabulary. She has rewritten her story. Her ending will not mirror her parents' ending. What she has, the willingness to rebound, they did not possess. What she has, any one of us can claim for ourselves. The choice is available. Choose wisely.

Further Reflection

Let's take a moment to recall an earlier time when we practiced one or two of the suggestions that were demonstrated in this chapter. And if you haven't made a practice of any of them yet, can you remember a situation that would have been a perfect opportunity to express resilience? If you were able to re-experience the circumstance and take advantage of the chance to practice resilience, what might it look like? Share your thoughts with a friend, or in a journal. We can only make something our own when we practice it and then tell someone else about it too. Forge ahead!

2

Choosing Perseverance

Every strike brings me closer to the next home run.

Babe Ruth

Perseverance is the key to success. Anyone's success. It's the dedication to move forward regardless of the odds against you, regardless of the mini-failures along the way. It's buckling down and saying, to yourself or sometimes to others too, *I can do this!* It's refusing to give up even when at first we don't succeed. Perseverance is resilience transformed into positive action. If resilience is the tool handed over by adversity, perseverance is the ongoing building project as you put those tools to work.

Perseverance is the absolute decision to stick to a goal in spite of setbacks. It's never giving up, even in the face of constant barriers. It's saying "yes" when all the signs around you point to "NO!"

The above quote strikes at the very heart of focused and fought-for success. The eventual overcoming of the dire circumstances that so many of us grew up in depends on perseverance. These are circumstances that bespeak certain failure, and yet millions rise above it. What is in their makeup that propels them forward in spite of the odds? For some I think it's sheer determination to "show them," particularly those who put us down so often. According to the dictionary, perseverance is "steadfastness in doing something despite difficulty or delay in achieving success." That describes Charlie, the pilot, to a tee.

Charlie's father couldn't bring himself to praise Charlie about anything. While it was true that Charlie did bring shame on himself and his family in his youth by way of some of his pranks, like the time he "accidentally" burned down the garage, he also accomplished many remarkable feats through his creativity. His dad overlooked these feats, unable to see beyond the disappointments.

One of the remarkable things Charlie shared with me, and the one example that reflects perseverance most, is the way he went about getting his first job as a pilot. And this was after the perseverance it took to complete all of his training and get every license that was possible for a pilot to attain, including two that are the Ph.D. of all aviation licenses: an Air Transport Pilot License and an Airframe and Powerplant License.

After completing his training, Charlie made hundreds of copies of his résumé and sent them to every airline large and small throughout the country. Then got in his car and headed west, visiting every regional airport he came to. He was turned away by more than one hundred, he said, but in every instance, he thanked the interviewer, telling them, "You are helping me get closer to the one who will finally say yes and offer me a job." Sure enough, that *one* finally beckoned. This story astounded me and it proves my point, and Babe Ruth's too, that no failure is the end; it's just a rung on the ladder of success.

....

Those who are successful decide, again and again, that they will not give up or give in to failure.

....

My own experience with writing a three-hundred-page dissertation taught me that committing to climb the spiral staircase every day and writing for four hours, one word at a time, could produce something remarkable. I wasn't a scholar, but I was committed to finishing what I had begun. Sticking with any project, regardless of its size or complexity, is what success is made of. I don't kid myself into thinking my particular dissertation was the best one ever submitted to an American Studies Ph.D. committee, but I think a good part of the committee's approval was based on my unrelenting commitment to finishing the degree I had begun. It was a labor of love, one to which each committee member also committed at an earlier time in his or her life.

Perseverance is about moving onward and upward regardless of the many boulders that roll in our way, or that are placed there by other "travelers" who, for their own ego-related reasons, want to hinder our success. Those competitors are real. They will trip us up, if we allow them to. Envy and fear push them to try to deter others from the success they lust after.

The many individuals I interviewed for this book display a hallmark of real achievement: they have not allowed the naysayers to successfully deter them. Many begin the journey, but surmounting the boulders is too daunting. Growing up in a dysfunctional home makes the path to success even more precarious. However, for those of us who travel this path through dysfunction and arrive at long-sought success, it is all the sweeter. Those you are reading about here are evidence.

Perseverance is applying ourselves to a task, over and over again, until we feel satisfied with the results.

Let me tell you now about Carl. He too succeeded, but not before dark clouds enveloped him many times. Like so many of us, he never lived up to his dad's dream. From childhood on, when he couldn't catch a ball that was tossed at him, or ride a bike when the other boys did, or read a book without stumbling over the words, his dad heaped shame on him. "What's the matter with you, you dummy?" was a common taunt. Carl said he cried regularly, but tried to hide his tears because they invited even more shame and more frequent teasing. Fortunately, Carl's mother soothed his feelings, but she didn't confront Dad. She, too, feared his derision.

Even though much later in life Carl came to understand his father's own fear of failure, his psyche had been wounded to the core. It stood in the way of his early attempts at success. He wasn't able to handle college work—not because he wasn't smart enough, but because he didn't have the courage it took to compete in that arena. He shared with me that he hadn't wanted to go to college right out of high school, and that he had one sister who pled his case with his dad. However, there was no reasonable discussion allowed. He was going. Period!

Carl began his downward slide in the first semester, and when he was dropped from the roster of those who were being considered for membership in a particular fraternity, he quit going to classes all together. His father's response wasn't kind. Nor was it fitting for the gravity of what Carl had just experienced—it minimized his pain. He said suicide didn't really attract him, but crawling under the covers and never coming out did. Fortunately he had a lovely girlfriend who was able to soften the blow he had experienced, and they married soon after.

Carl continued to live in the shadow of his father, a shadow that engulfed him in both shame and anxiety. His father watched his movements on the job like a hawk, even though they didn't even work for the same company. Whenever Carl failed to be at his desk on time, a piece of information his dad knew because he drove by Carl's office on his own way to work, he'd call and criticize him for being lazy and undependable.

Finally Carl quit going to work, much like he'd quit going to classes. His boss paid a visit, apologetically fired him, and then suggested Carl move away so his dad could hound him no longer. And in fact, that's exactly what he did, with a great letter of recommendation from his boss. He finally got his chance to shine, to persevere, and he did. He became a supervisor, and his employees appreciated his many kindnesses. He knew so well how disrespect felt, and he wasn't interested in going down that dark alley with his employees.

Perseverance is being steadfast, not letting failure deter you from staying committed to the goal.

Carl was steadily employed his whole life, retiring only recently, and was honored by his employer and by those he supervised when he left. He could hold his head high. He had learned that perseverance paid off. He knew, firsthand, the pain of criticism contrasted with the pleasure of success. And his experiences prepared him to be an exemplary father to his own children. They never had reason to doubt themselves. He was there to support them at every turn, encouraging them whenever they faltered. His own youth had served him well, if only by way of contrast. He knew what he didn't want his own children to have to experience, and they excelled in every way, just as he excelled as their father.

One of the upsides of being beaten down is that in response, sensitive people will cringe at the thought of beating anyone else down. Some, of course, will pass on to others that which they were made to experience, and many people don't know how to do anything else. But if the receiver has a loving buffer, like the wife Carl was so fortunate to have, he or she will learn and be able to practice another way of relating to the outside world.

Perseverance isn't accomplished as a single act. The beauty of Carl's story is the moment when he relocated at the suggestion of his boss. This represented a breakthrough in his search for a life that was different in every way from the one he experienced with his father close at hand. This was a courageous decision, the first of many he was to make that solidified his success in a life separate from the family that deadened his spirit. Perseverance may start with a single act, but it is ongoing and requires one's full attention. Fortunately, the payoff begins right away, making it all the easier to stay the course.

Another young woman I interviewed comes to mind. Her name is Valerie, and she survived—I use this term intentionally—one of the most dysfunctional families I was introduced to while doing research for this book. Valerie grew up in a small town in northern Minnesota.

She was the youngest of four children. Both parents were drug-using alcoholics. And neither mother nor father truly parented the children. Fortunately, the grandparents stepped in.

How Valerie became so resilient and successfully persevered, creating a full and very successful life as a bilingual teacher, is a marvel to be privy to. Her deftness at navigating around and through the myriad landmines set within her family over the years quite literally changed my perception of the possibilities for overcoming what appeared to be "intentional abuse." Many would have succumbed to a life of drinking and drug abuse themselves. The pills and the alcohol were certainly within easy reach for Valerie's entire young life. She saw going to college as an escape, she said. She didn't plan for a life beyond college. Nor did she really anticipate what college would be like. She simply knew she had to escape her family of origin if she was to live.

....

Perseverance is not a single act. It's ongoing.

....

Perseverance beckons whenever we are involved in an activity that fully engages us. This was true for Valerie. She discovered her love of language and her facility with learning another tongue. The excitement she felt helped to obliterate some of the pain of abandonment she felt nearly every day upon arriving home from school, and the pain of hunger at mealtime with no parent in sight. Seeking help from counselors, which she fortunately did when she went to college, got her over many bumps in the road. However, more than once she flirted with suicide during her college years.

The past clings unless we can comfortably put it to bed, and that takes effort. When our attention is shifted from our past dysfunctional surroundings and placed on ourselves and our own journey, miracles seem to happen. It's not an unusual response by a family to seek relief from their own addictions. Others in our lives deserve the freedom to make their own journey while we make ours. Indeed, this is the freedom everyone must have if we are to become who we were born to be.

When I reflect on perseverance and the many gifts it bestows on us, I'm reminded of Harry. He was a drug addict from an early age. We can't really blame addiction on our family of origin, regardless of our desire to do so when we first get clean and sober, but Harry's family was extremely dysfunctional. Choosing to get high, rather than relate to them, seemed like a good choice.

Harry's older brother was mentally ill and institutionalized on many occasions. His parents raged at each other and the boys. Harry was not a good student, not for lack of a good mind but because he lacked direction and focus. As soon as he was introduced to heroin, he spent more time in a stupor than in class.

When I first met Harry we were both new in recovery. He was a charmer, like so many drug addicts are. But he was learning to leave the manipulation in the past. Manipulation is a default position for so many who have lived on the edge with alcoholism and drug addiction. (I didn't escape its allure either.) Once you find success by manipulating others, it's hard not to turn to it, again and again. Harry had been a master, but he didn't want to live in that arena anymore. He was intent on changing. And in time, he did.

Perseverance is oftentimes doing more than is expected.

But let me turn to Harry's perseverance. When we met, he was a server in a restaurant. It was a high-end establishment, and his charm worked wonders. It earned him big tips and the attention of the owner, who soon made him the supervisor of all the servers. He loved the attention and the opportunity this presented. He took the job seriously and began to see where changes could be made in how the restaurant functioned. Before long, he moved into management and became the right-hand person to the owners. His perseverance paid off in spades. They looked to him as a problem solver and a visionary, and he loved the attention he earned and the monetary rewards too.

Working for others in the restaurant business lost its luster after a few years, so Harry formed a partnership with a friend, one he thought he knew well, and they opened their own establishment. No matter how hard Harry worked, he couldn't make the business pay off. What he didn't realize until well into the second year was that his partner was skimming from the profits. Harry's side of the business was to manage the staff and the kitchen. His partner, a man who had business acumen, was in charge of the expenses and the revenues. The balance sheet simply didn't add up.

By the time Harry fully realized the extent of the problem, the creditors and the IRS were knocking on their door. Many people would have filed bankruptcy and walked away. Harry had far too much pride and honesty to do that. They got themselves into the mess, so they needed to do the honorable thing and manage to find the money to pay off their debts. After closing the doors,

Harry's partner disappeared, but Harry began the long journey back to solvency. He could have made excuses, blamed his former partner, and hung his head in shame. Instead, he got another job and began paying the IRS and the other creditors what they were owed. He persevered. One foot in front of the other, year in and year out, until the books were balanced. This was his goal, and eventually he made good on every last penny owed.

In the process, he realized he needed another profession that paid more, and he went back to school. That was a wise decision. He learned the finer points of computer science, including web design, and started his own business. He successfully manages that company today. What he doesn't know, he figures out; nothing is too daunting for his inquisitive mind. Nothing is so overwhelming that one who perseveres can't rise above it. Harry is a great case in point, as are Carl, Charlie, and me, too.

Perseverance is learning to rely on the successful examples of others. These individuals are not on one's path accidentally.

When people like us are confronted with what looks like the impossible, we turn to the resources we have mastered. For some it's prayer and meditation. For others it's seeking the guidance of friends, counselors, and mentors— even going to the Internet for clues. The important point here is that perseverance is a tool and a gift to be appreciated when one sees the effectiveness of its application. Never giving up is the underlying key, always.

Before moving on, let's reiterate some of the key points regarding perseverance. If you need encouragement to persevere, perhaps these few reminders will give you the boost you need:

Those who are successful simply decide, again and again, that they will not give up or give in. Determination is what they have.

They rely on the successful examples of others in their lives—individuals who are there for a reason. *Lest we forget, no one is on our path accidentally!*

They discover that our teachers are always present to help us see what our next step should be.

In most instances perseverance means simply to apply ourselves to a task, over and over again, until we feel satisfied with the results. We won't be perfect in our efforts the first time, or even the last. Perfection isn't our goal. Perseverance is, and it's attainable.

It's ongoing. Not a single act.

Perseverance is oftentimes doing more than what's expected.

It requires full attention for the long haul, but the payoff begins immediately.

And finally, it's being steadfast, not letting failure deter you from staying committed to the goal.

Further Reflection

Take some time to share in a journal or with a friend some of your experiences with this trait. If you have too few successes with it so far, can you see where you might have made good use of it? Can you take a few moments, now, to "re-vision" the situation, living it more successfully? This will help to create the habit of living this way more often.

Both resilience and perseverance can feel like a heavy load, a long trek over rocky terrain. But neither can be accomplished effectively without what we're going to explore in the next chapter: a sense of humor. Having a sense of humor lightens anyone's load. And those of us who grew up in dysfunctional homes have realized, as perhaps few others do, the value of being able to laugh at our past and our exaggerated reactions to it. Let's turn to those examples now.

3

Relishing a Sense of Humor

A well-developed sense of humor is the pole that adds balance to the tightrope you walk throughout your life.

William Arthur Ward

Every person I interviewed for this book had been forced to walk a tightrope in their family of origin. Remarkably, each and every one of them displayed a good sense of humor. Because they successfully survived families marked by extreme dysfunction—families that appeared unconsciously intent on destroying the lives of every family member—these individuals clung to the life raft of humor, finding ways to laugh when the slightest opportunity presented itself. It takes a special willingness to shift one's perception, to see whatever is before you in a new light. A sense of humor is often the key as "survivors" learn to not only make the best of a situation but to turn it into an advantage. Being able to smile at how stuck you were previously lightens one's load in the moment. My own experience has shown me that it lightens one's load for the long haul too.

What does this sense of humor look and feel like? What comes first to my mind is that deep belly laugh that erupts within us, often over the silliest things—perhaps something kind of dumb that a friend or even a small child says. It's being able to identify with the many humorous situations in sitcoms, or better yet, stage plays. It's being tickled by cartoons in a magazine like *The New Yorker*. And sometimes we laugh deeply just because . . . We might not know what triggers the laughter. We simply know it feels good. It feels freeing. Some have said that we are closer to God when we laugh than at any other time. No way to prove that, of course, but laughter is good because it "right-sizes" us—it shifts our perception and we sense the clarity, the gift of real "vision," instantly.

A sense of humor can be cultivated.

We know that a sense of humor can make life more tolerable, but how might it affect the outcome of a dire circumstance? I can best explain this through an example. Dawn, the Native American woman I referred to in an earlier chapter, had every reason to be discouraged to the point of suicide—a choice made by a number of her siblings as well as her father. She generally shrugged her shoulders at the problems that mounted in her life, and there were many. She used drugs and alcohol to excess for a number of years as a way of coping, but after finally attaining sobriety, which eluded her more than once (I'd have to guess twenty or thirty times, in fact), she turned more and more to laughter. She enjoyed her own and also enjoyed inspiring it in others.

She lived on the edge for decades. She survived her many death-defying encounters with alcohol and drugs, and this convinced her that living on the edge was doable. In fact, she regularly proclaimed that if you weren't living on the edge, you were taking up too much space. She chuckled every time she said it. We did too, hearing her and knowing what she meant.

We always have a choice regarding how we will see any situation, whether from the past or this moment.

Dawn showed me that if you could maintain a sense of humor in spite of living through circumstances like hers, seeing the funny side of life was perhaps a gift unlike any other. In a group, her sense of humor gave a lift to the experiences of so many of us, proving that only one in a crowd had to see the funny side to open it up for many to be able to see it in time.

Humor has been credited with healing many ills. I remember reading Norman Cousins's book *Anatomy of an Illness*, in which he shared how he had used laughter to heal himself of cancer. It was a remarkable story. It stands as a great example of the power of laughter in our lives no matter what circumstance has caused us pain: emotional, physical, or mental—even all three. He insisted that a good belly laugh every day was just what the doctor ordered. It may well be the very thing that has kept Dawn alive far beyond what her friends and family had expected. Laughter certainly contributed to Judith's survival too.

I mentioned Judith in an earlier chapter, but there was much about her life that I didn't share at that time, and much that I will share later in the book too. For now let me say she was a potential suicide victim throughout much of her life. She said thoughts of suicide began while she was a youngster, not because she wanted to punish others, which is one of the explanations psychologists often use; that didn't even occur to her. She just wanted to escape the pain of life and didn't really think her suicidal thoughts were a big deal. Even into adulthood she harbored these thoughts, sometimes making carefully laid out plans. When a counselor told her mentally healthy people didn't contemplate suicide, she didn't believe her.

When she was early in recovery, Judith's last bona fide plan to kill herself was just moments from being executed. She was saved by an unexpected visitor, a total stranger in fact, knocking on her door. This struck her as both a miracle and almost laughable, especially since the visitor insisted the visit had been arranged many weeks before.

....

We can't entertain more than one thought at a time. Choose to let whatever thought you entertain be one that creates an inner chuckle or a good belly laugh whenever possible.

....

Judith was quick to laugh at herself. She hadn't laughed much as a child in her tense family, she said; no one did. But as someone relatively new to recovery, she began to see the humorous side of many situations. Whenever the opportunity to laugh presented itself in the recovery rooms she frequented, she relished her deep-throated laughter. Luckily, recovering alcoholics are pretty quick to laugh at themselves. Judith also shared how grateful she is that she married someone who makes her laugh every day, and she is convinced that this adds value not only to her recovery but to all the interactions she has with everyone else.

I'm convinced that the pain of one's earlier life is lessened a tiny bit by each moment of laughter we allow ourselves to experience. And I know that when I laugh, whatever I am doing gets easier to handle. Bringing laughter with you wherever you go benefits human kind. Psychologists and psychiatrists everywhere agree with this. Laughter is like a dose of medicine for the soul. It quiets, soothes, and lifts up the soul.

What is it about having a sense of humor that makes such a difference in the journey we are on? What comes to mind first is that *we simply can't entertain two thoughts at one time.* If what we are thinking is lightening our load, or better yet, giving us a good chuckle, we are discarding another thought that's causing a dark cloud to hover over the path we are traveling. We can choose one thought or the other. And we can make the choice many times in a day. That's the good news. A few bad, cloudy hours can be lightened by laughter in the blink of an eye. It's happened to me thousands of times.

Make the decision to spend time every day with people who make you laugh. It's good for your soul.

This reminds me of laughter yoga, a phenomenon that is popular in many countries throughout the world, and in the past couple of years is being practiced in the United States too. It's the brainchild of Dr. Madan Kataria, a physician from Mumbai, India. According to the Internet, he launched the first Laughter Club at a park on March 13, 1995, along with a handful of people. Today, it has become a worldwide phenomenon with more than six thousand Social Laughter Clubs in about sixty countries.

People I know who have tried laughter yoga are pretty amazed at its effectiveness. What does it accomplish? As I just stated, we can't entertain two expressions or thoughts at any one time. If we are experiencing a moment of full-throated laughter, we can't be focusing on a negative idea. Practitioners of laughter yoga say it actually changes brain chemistry, and thereby changes perception. And that changes our life, too.

Newcomers to the recovery process are often surprised by all of the laughter in AA meetings. And considering the trauma so many of us have lived through, it perhaps does seem unusual, even macabre, to the untutored. However, being able to laugh at ourselves, the insanity of our past behavior, and the horrors of growing up in families that were often filled with abusive outbursts, is truly the healing balm that allows us to know *we are going to be okay.* Not a single person I interviewed felt he or she was okay as a youngster. Most felt terrified and unable to cope successfully with life well into adulthood, and yet every one of them laughed heartily many times as we talked.

....

Our willingness to laugh is the first necessary step.

....

Charlie, the pilot whose story we covered earlier, was such a great example of the laughter payoff. He was a prankster as a youngster and continues to be one. It was a joy to interview him. In fact, throughout our conversations we laughed a great deal. Nothing in particular seemed to precipitate it. It just erupted so naturally. The willingness we both had for "living into" the lighter expression of life opened my heart to the laughter that heals.

Charlie grew up in an insane household, but eventually embraced a solid recovery. One of ten children with an alcoholic, workaholic dad and a martyred, very devout Catholic mother, Charlie learned to rely on no one and to create his own reality. His reality included making fun of others, playing practical jokes, and hiding his feelings in his creativity. He rebuilt wagons, bicycles, radios, and anything else that captured his attention, particularly those things that appeared to need refurbishing. He was great at taking something and making it better, he said. He kept busy in this way, which saved him from much heartache in a family that paid him little attention.

He also had discovered at an early age that he could so easily, so naturally make others laugh. He relied on that skill as a way to "get over" with the girls when he was young. He did this with his family too. For one of his memorable pranks, on the occasion of a sibling's birthday, he fell flat on a boxed birthday cake he was carrying up the basement stairs into the kitchen. Unbeknownst to everyone, Charlie had removed the cake before tripping on the top step and falling on the box, and he got a huge round of laughter and applause. It's a memory others in the family still recall.

So many I interviewed developed the skill of creating laughter in the midst of situations that were more likely to be marred by alcoholic outbursts than by joyful ones. Pranks and joke telling were diversionary tools that many tried to master. It kept the attention away from whoever might prefer to cause trouble as the result of drinking too much. And there were always those who drank too much. My interviewees often drank too much themselves, but when given the opportunity, getting others to laugh often took precedence.

So far we have talked about resilience, perseverance, and now a sense of humor as specific examples of "the good stuff" that can be cultivated by those who have been raised in dysfunctional families. I'm inclined to say that the offspring of dysfunctional homes may be the luckiest of all the members of the human community. They have highly developed abilities to survive and even thrive in whatever situation plucks them from the crowd.

Carl, so maligned by his critical father, comes to mind once again. He had the heartiest laugh, perhaps most of all the people I interviewed. And no other person I was able to talk with had more criticism heaped on him while growing up. He was humiliated for decades but had risen above it and displayed not only a superior sense of humor but also a softness that comforted anyone who was drawn to him. He embodied love even though very little love was openly bestowed on him as a youngster or even young adult.

While it is often said that we can only give to others what we have received ourselves, we don't necessarily get "the good stuff" from our family of origin. Wherever we discover it, we can make use of it. And I find it interesting, too, that we are capable of transforming the negative into the positive by sheer determination. My interviewees demonstrated this capability tenfold.

Before moving into the next section, let's close this chapter, like the previous ones, with a simple overview:

A sense of humor can be cultivated.

We always have a choice regarding how we will see any situation, whether it's from our past or this moment.

We can't entertain more than one thought at a time; let the thought you choose create an inner chuckle or a good belly laugh whenever possible.

Make the decision to spend time every day with people who make you laugh. It's good for your soul.

Make a point of seeing a comedy, occasionally. Norman Cousins gave us a powerful message in this regard in *Anatomy of an Illness.*

Make a humor list, similar to a gratitude list, at the end of every day for a week or two. Keep track of all the experiences that made you laugh out loud or even smile. The more we remember these episodes, the more we will help to create them for others too. Read the list whenever you are feeling out of sorts.

Make a point of meditating daily, even for five minutes, about a humorous experience that recently happened. Observe how it changes your demeanor.

Our willingness to laugh is the first necessary step. We all know sour pusses. We don't ever have to be one.

Every day is a new day. Make the decision to laugh often. It will change your life.

Cherish the humor in cartoons—those we receive in emails and those we come across in magazines like *The New Yorker.* They can change the tenor of the day, instantly.

Further Reflection

Take a few minutes to review some of the times, recently, when you let laughter change how you felt in a particular situation. Also, think of a time when you could have responded with some humor but opted to stay stuck in a sour mood. If you could change that experience, how would it look?

In the first three chapters, we have covered three significant characteristics that are keys to successfully overcoming the dark past that hounded so many of us. But there is more. Let's turn next to forgiveness and the profound power it wields in our lives.

4

Forgiving the Past and Growing Into the Present

There is no love without forgiveness, and there is no forgiveness without love.

Bryant H. McGill

What is the miracle of forgiveness? How does it measure up as a miracle? First let me say that forgiving is perhaps the most important action we will ever take within the many relationships we cherish. Forgiveness can free us from the past: by letting someone off the hook for a bona fide putdown or other action that felt demeaning, or even a suspected action that we are obsessing over, or in many other ways. For instance, willingness to forgive a betrayal can seem unfathomable when first considered, but the release it offers us as soon as we have forgiven the perpetrator is palpable. The importance of forgiveness, of any action by another—lying, stealing, even the horror of sexual abuse—simply can't be overestimated. Until we let go of the very real or imagined transgressions of others, we will know no peace. None whatsoever!

To repeat, it's hard to overestimate the power of forgiveness. This isn't the first time that I have written about the importance of forgiveness. In fact, I have shared my personal experiences with forgiveness myriad times in other books while recounting my growth in the many significant relationships throughout my life. I have been convinced for many years that *without forgiveness, we simply don't grow.* But we also don't stay stationary. Without forgiveness, we regress step by step, relationship by relationship. And what a sorry existence we have if we resist the opportunity to forgive ourselves and all the real or imagined attackers in our life.

....

Forgiveness by one person heals many.

....

I assure you that forgiveness is a gift—one that continues to bless us and all the many individuals we encounter every day of our lives. Many would say it's the only gift that never stops giving because of how it changes who we are, how we think, and every action we take. When we hang on to the past and refuse to forgive whatever the many resentments or judgments might be, we not only hold ourselves back from life's joys, but we cling to any and all past experiences we felt sure were meant to destroy us. Not a single one of them, *regardless of the circumstance that gave rise to it*, is or ever was worth holding us hostage for a lifetime, or even for a day.

I have become convinced that the true value of forgiveness comes from the way in which it weaves two individuals together. We become *joined* with those people we forgive, and that's where healing is birthed, theirs and ours. The separation we had curried heretofore gives way, and our hearts become one. We can actually feel the transformation as it's taking place. It's an inner shift, sometimes slight, but at the same time, quietly profound. Always. In some circles this is referred to as *a holy instant*.

Forgiveness closes the gap between all of us.

Forgiving *ourselves* for our judgments of others (and for most of us, judgment is all too common) may be even more important for healing. When we are willing to cultivate a truly forgiving heart, healing becomes the underlying theme of every encounter we experience every day. Though it may sound daunting to cultivate such a heart, this challenge will continue to entice us once we have experienced even the slightest gift that it produces.

When interviewing the many men and women for this book, I found that the act of forgiveness played a key role in their lives, too. As I have already discussed, forgiveness of others, as well as ourselves, shifts our perception of every moment. That's where the miracle lies. When we allow ourselves to let go of anger, resentment, or judgment, and simply rest in the act of forgiveness, the resulting shift in perception lessens the heaviness of our lives. We simply can't appreciate how freeing life feels until we have embraced forgiveness. Nor can we make the most of any present moment if we have not embraced forgiveness of the past.

Forgiveness is perhaps the kindest, most loving act we can ever perform.

Our lives are indeed undeniably changed when we let ourselves hear how others have been changed too. William, the avid reader with the distant father and the volatile mother, didn't want to forgive his parents. His very neurotic, angry mother and emotionally distant father molded him in such a way that for him to reach out to anyone, or be touched by any other, emotionally or even physically, was seldom appreciated or sought as a nurturing gesture. He shared with me that he had never considered forgiveness to have any value until after he began to work a twelve-step program, which he entered solely because of his wife's alcoholism. In each of the circles that invited him in, many gifts gradually came to William as he became willing to quietly listen to the stories of others, gathering the wisdom of all those who shared their experiences with forgiveness.

As William explained it, nothing looks the same to him now. Absolutely nothing. And even though he may not be entirely forgiving of his parents—yet—he can allow the past to be what it was, accepting that his parents did the best they could with what they had been taught about survival and parenting. He can claim the benefits of today and the growth he has garnered as the result of what he has learned about forgiveness from other twelve steppers. He knows this has helped him as a parent, a role he treasures, and as a more understanding husband. And he can finally see alcoholism as a disease, not as an attack on him or a weakness in his wife.

The universe shifts when we take on forgiveness as an assignment.

One of the joys in my interview with William was his sincere gratitude for all he has learned since becoming "teachable." He had considered himself very self-sufficient and had prided himself on not really needing the input of anyone. After all, he was well educated and was raised to be independent and very self-reliant. Now he truly relishes what he learns from the many others he now proudly walks among. His attention to what the others around him are saying serves as a great example to the newcomers who have come to the recovery rooms.

It doesn't matter where we learn the finer points of forgiveness. Learning them is what's important. However, one thing is for certain: it's the blending of all the experiences of one's past that brings us to the threshold of willingness to finally seek another way to live. Every part of William's past—his cold, Scandinavian upbringing; his dangerously neurotic mother and his emotionally unavailable dad; the untimely death of his first wife; the alcoholism of his second wife—combined to ready him to receive the tools of forgiveness. Seeing life, his own and others, from a fresh perspective gave him hope that his future could be whatever he wanted it to be. It wasn't set in stone as he had once imagined it was.

....

Forgiveness has an inherent power that is life-sustaining and everlasting. Life never feels the same once we have truly practiced forgiveness.

....

Valerie, the astonishingly resilient young woman who survived great odds in her family of origin, has had to become very practiced at forgiveness too. As mentioned earlier, she was parented, if you could call it that, by two actively alcoholic and drug-addicted parents. She was the youngest of four children and were it not for her grandparents, she might not have survived the trauma of her existence. She certainly could not count on either parent to guide her or be available for her, emotionally or physically; nor could she count on them even being home when she returned from school. But because her grandparents were aware of her home life, she did get fed, she did have clean clothes, and she wasn't left alone during the long nights. She and her siblings could call on one grandparent or the other, and help came.

Unfortunately, Valerie paid dearly for the lack of parenting. Although she never developed a dependence on alcohol or pills, as had been the case with both parents and one sister, she did develop severe anxiety, which crippled her emotionally for many years. Her battle with anxiety will never be completely won, she assumes, but she does function comfortably now with the help of medication, talk therapy, and meditation. She is quite convinced that her eventual willingness to accept that her parents did the best they could has made her growth possible.

Valerie didn't develop the willingness to forgive unaided, however. Most of us don't. That she did forgive them has made her far more accepting of all people, which in turn lessens her anxiety. It's interesting how we get payoffs in many respects, in other areas of our lives and in relationships, when we strengthen the practice of forgiveness. Being willing to fully forgive in one relationship improves our level of acceptance of everyone we encounter. And that's the direct result of the changed heart that is the ultimate gift of forgiveness. Imagine a specific example: that coworker who drives you crazy or the friend who is always complaining about relatively inane problems can be overlooked with greater ease, or even quietly blessed, once you have become a practitioner of forgiveness.

....

Forgiveness isn't limited in its reward to only the person who is forgiving the perceived adversary. It spills over and brings comfort to all relationships.

....

Let's review for a moment before going any further. What does forgiveness look and feel like? Based on my experience, I'd say it does not look or feel the same in every instance, but it will always have a softness about it. It will always draw formerly disparate souls together. It will send forth a healing balm to anyone who is close at hand. Even those who are miles away and unaware of the particulars of the forgiving act will be touched. Some call it the butterfly effect—a generally accepted fact of quantum physics that every action, large or microscopic, has a consequence; each of those consequences in turn creates another consequence and another, *ad infinitum*.

Forgiveness cannot be contained. It fully permeates a moment, and then it reaches far beyond that moment. I have come to image the "give" portion of for-***give***-ness as the heart opening up to the former adversary and saying, in its own way, "let's close this gap between us forevermore." And by extension, gaps then close between other people too.

I do think that we break hearts when we refuse to forgive—our own, and others'. We mend them when we listen to the ever-present inner call. Each person I spoke with agreed at some point to listen to that inner call, and their life was transformed. In that process many other lives were transformed too.

A decision to embrace forgiveness creates its own momentum.

Let's return to Valerie's experience. Her mother made a commitment to recover from her own addictions, and this led to Valerie's willingness to forgive her parents, particularly her mother (her father died while she was still young). Even though her mother was a bit slow to make amends, her children were patient, particularly Valerie. Her life remained troubled for a time. She was in the hospital for anxiety, depression, and suicidal tendencies on more than one occasion, but she has stayed the course, and continues to make forward progress. And she has made a commitment to self-improvement, which has included inventorying the past and making the effort to lead always from a place of love in all her relationships. This led to a kind of softness, which is one of the benefits, really, of embracing forgiveness. It softens us as it softens those around us. Love is more easily expressed when the heart is soft.

I don't want to imply that we must live in totally dysfunctional families in order to reap the benefits that accrue from forgiveness, but at least we can find benefit from having survived those families, and that's worth rejoicing over. Forgiveness is one of those life-altering expressions, and if the only way we can claim the reward is to suffer the dysfunction first, so be it.

I return to Carl, the hard worker with the abusive father, again because I was so moved by his struggle. Even though he did finally get to a place of forgiveness, it wasn't before his father passed on. And I'm not sure he has yet to reap the full benefit of it. You can still see the sadness in his face and feel it in his demeanor. The pain of his upbringing because he didn't meet his father's expectations was profound. His father was a perfectionist personified. He ridiculed Carl throughout his young life. As I mentioned in an earlier chapter, he didn't even stop after Carl left home and married. And even though Carl moved away to escape the constant criticism, it left an indelible mark. Was Carl's father a mean man? Not really, Carl said.

He was simply as hard on his son as he was on himself, and no one can match the expectations of a perfectionist.

Forgiveness heals the aching heart like nothing else.

The truly unfortunate thing about Carl's experiences was the manner in which they molded his self-esteem. To say he had low self-esteem for most of his life would be an understatement. The saving grace, he said, was his marriage to a woman who loved him dearly, for his failings as well as his few successes. He and his wife had two children and he excelled as a father. He attempted to be everything his father was incapable of being. His heart just wouldn't allow him to do to his children what had been done to him. He lovingly showed up, in every way imaginable. And he learned to let his own past be over.

Whether Carl went as far as true forgiveness of his dad, I couldn't say, but he did begin to understand that his dad had been a tortured soul. And that lessened the impact of how his dad had behaved. He came to understand that his dad's treatment wasn't truly personal, but rather reflected his own low self-esteem. We do such unkindnesses to others because of how we feel about ourselves, and these unkindnesses continue to happen among friends, strangers, in families, and in the workplace. How we see ourselves is how we see others. The treatment follows suit. And the die is cast. Over and over, the die is cast.

We can be introduced to the blessing of forgiveness, however. We can listen to the stories of others, their experiences, and then dare to practice forgiving others too. That's what William has done. Valerie learned the value of forgiveness by practicing it after a bit of coaching from her therapist. And with Carl, his wife set the example. She knew because of her own healed heart that Carl could heal too. And she showed him how. As his demeanor is still a bit sad, perhaps there is still work to be done, but the timeline is open. The benefits will wait for Carl and any of the rest of us who journey to a better tomorrow. The benefits will wait for as long as it takes.

Before moving on to the next "opportunity" these interviewees and I were able to glean from our dysfunctional rearing, let's review what we have learned about forgiveness:

Forgiveness closes the gap between us, *all of us.*

It is a decision, first, that creates its own momentum.

It's an act that doesn't limit its reward to just the person who is forgiving the perceived adversary. It spills over and brings comfort to all relationships, as when a pebble thrown into the water sends ripples that travel outward for a long time.

Forgiveness heals the individual, the family, the community, the universe. Does this seem unrealistic? Think again.

Forgiveness by one person heals many.

The forgiveness we offer others returns to us tenfold.

Forgiveness offers loving closure in all relationships.

Seeking the guidance of one's Higher Power makes forgiveness an easy offering.

Forgiveness is quite possibly the kindest, most loving act we can ever perform.

Forgiveness heals the aching heart like nothing else.

Some think that our greatest act is to forgive, both ourselves and others.

The universe will shift when we all take on forgiveness as our assignment.

If you have not forgiven your adversaries yet, today is the day to begin.

Forgiveness has an inherent power that is life sustaining and everlasting. Life never feels the same once we have truly practiced forgiveness.

Further Reflection

Who have you forgiven so far? How did it change you? How did it change the relationship? Was any other relationship altered too? Who is on your list to forgive? Consider making a plan, now, for how and when you will approach him or her. This will not only offer you relief but it will begin the heart-softening process. After the plan is made, write a paragraph or two about how you feel.

5

Surrendering the Need to Win

Something amazing happens when we surrender and just love. We melt into another world, a realm of power already within us. The world changes when we change. The world softens when we soften. The world loves us when we choose to love the world.

Marianne Williamson

When we practice stepping aside, letting *what is, be*, rather than bulldozing our way over or through the situations that have drawn our attention, we allow life to flow smoothly forward. Surrendering to the uncontrollable, (and all things separate from us are uncontrollable) rather than insisting our opinions; our way of doing tasks; our outlook on life, particularly on how others should see life too; is a peace-filled choice. Actually, it's the only reasonable choice.

I never saw surrender in a positive way in my family of origin. Never. My father was ALWAYS RIGHT! No matter what the conversation entailed and no matter who was involved, there were no compromises to be made with him. My life has markedly improved since embracing the idea of surrender. And my life is far more peaceful too. As Marianne says in the above quote, something amazing indeed does happen when we give up or give in, when we let go and release.

Surrendering is a magical experience. To surrender changes every moment we live. It changes every experience, every person, every plan or dream we might have. It changes every detail of the life that is intentionally moving toward us. How thrilling it is to contemplate the many gifts surrender makes possible.

As I have said in other chapters and in other books, my father's life was ruled by fear, and fear made him insistent on being the authority no matter what the situation or topic of discussion was. Growing up this way wasn't fun. It didn't inspire creative discourse, nor did it model how best to get along in the larger world. Unfortunately, we do take what we observed in the home outside of it, so for many years I mimicked him in my encounters with friends and even strangers. As a result, I wasn't all that fun to be around. I didn't even begin to embrace the idea of surrendering. I couldn't have even explained what it really meant or how it might feel. All I knew was that giving in was not for me.

It has been a long, oftentimes arduous journey traveling from *there to here*, but the peace I now feel on a daily basis is the gift of learning there is another way to navigate through life—a way that is far more accommodating to the soul, mine and everyone else's too. It's called surrendering; I see it as another word for love. It's a letting go, a letting down of the barriers, a release of the struggle to hold on to what was. It's freedom, clearly and simply. It's joy, absolutely.

It was my own dark struggle with alcohol, drugs, and men that ultimately led me to this place of peace on a daily installment. There can be a silver lining in every experience. My life is proof of that. I won't say I didn't stub my toes many times getting here. Change is never easy; nor is it even appealing when we first attempt it. And I had to change absolutely everything! When you think there is only one way to see life, *your way,* your resistance to change can be especially daunting. Incrementally it began to happen for me. And with each tiny change, each experience with surrendering, I could see the payoffs mounting.

To surrender means to let go, to release. It promises freedom to breathe deeply again.

The tutelage of others proved mandatory for me to grow, but I had resisted learning from others all my life. I recall how hard my dad had struggled to convince me to see life his way. He failed, of course. Our dance of discord lasted for many years. Fortunately, as my life changed, so did our dance. Being introduced to tools for living free from alcohol and drugs, free from constant fear and anxiety, free from the ennui that had followed me into the rooms by the many who were living lives of much greater ease—all this gave me hope. For the first time I found real hope that my life could truly be experienced on a higher, more peaceful plane.

I resisted changing at first, but I was attracted to how much easier life seemed to be for some of my new friends, and I wanted what they had. They informed me that I had to surrender to get there. This meant I had to surrender my attempts to control other people's lives. I had to learn an entirely new response to the many situations that I felt sure were screaming for my control. The new friends reminded me that my control wasn't needed or wanted by anyone. One really good friend often said, "There are two kinds of business, Karen. Your business and none of your business." Hearing this was my cue to surrender.

It felt so foreign at first, but it's amazing how good surrender feels to me now. After years of living in dysfunction, surrender initially feels like a cowardly act, particularly if one parent was a bully of sorts. It might seem to us that surrender allows others to walk all over us. My search for tools that would perfect my skills at control led me to a twelve-step recovery room. The first time I saw the slogan *Let Go and Let God* in one of these rooms, I doubted that I'd find what I was looking for in that setting. Learning how to *let go* seemed ludicrous. I had set some big goals, and how was I going to accomplish them if I just let go? But indeed, that was the whole point of the recovery process.

Perhaps I got tired of being in a state of conflict all the time. The inner tension was exhausting. Surrendering became easier the more I practiced it. It became more appealing too. I am sharing more of my own story in this chapter than in some others because of the profound impact this practice has had on my life, all my relationships, my worldview, and my chosen work. Being willing to surrender—giving up control over the lives of others (which we can't control anyway) and simply enjoying the fruits of my own life has given me immeasurable pleasure. It has given me a yearning to encourage others to live likewise. And now I know I can encourage them by example only, not by control.

....

Surrendering is what invites God to drive the limousine we are riding in.

....

Let me describe just how surrender looks. It can take many forms. It may be a simple smile at the assumed adversary. It may be a comment like "You might be right." It may be a soft silence. Perhaps it's a nod of the head. It sidesteps a rebuttal that can lead to an unnecessary conflict, and, in reality, all conflicts are unnecessary. We will inevitably fail in our attempts to control others, in one way or another, so surrendering this impulse is all that makes sense. When it becomes your daily practice, surrendering begins to feel like a breath of fresh air coupled with the release of the tightness in your shoulders or your chest. I know. It has become my path. My practice. My prayer.

Surrendering has changed every relationship I cherish. It even has the power to change the fleeting relationships in my day. The angry store clerk, the tailgating driver, the bickering neighbors can all be "sent on their way" with a nod of the head or shrug of the shoulders and a quietly spoken blessing.

I have had the good fortune to meet, make friends with, and interview numerous people who sing the praises of surrender as a principle for more peaceful living. I think that, unknowingly, I have begun to surround myself with folks who cherish surrender with as much gusto as I do. It's transforming in remarkable ways. I'll introduce you to a few of them in this chapter. Cecelia comes quickly to mind because she has had to practice the principle religiously with so many individuals in her life.

Let me begin with her family of origin. It was probably no different from many dysfunctional families in the way its members interfered, or tried to interfere, in Cecelia's life. But her commitment to the practice of surrender, which she had glommed on to in a twelve-step group, had to be constant if she was to have any serenity at all. Her father was an alcoholic and a philanderer, bringing his lovers into their home on occasion. Her mother was sickly, no doubt for legitimate reasons, but also probably because of the sadness that filled her heart because of the life she shared with her husband, a life that left her empty and mostly alone.

And then there were the differing political and philosophical views. Cecelia's father was adamant in his views, as so many of us are. He intended to be heard and supported if you lived under his roof. If you didn't share his party dogma, he expected you to be silent, expressing no opinion whatsoever. Cecelia, like so many young people, was educated to think differently from the moment she entered college. Her visits home, from that day forward, were fraught with tension, loud arguments, even physical violence on occasion. Her mother looked on, scared for her daughter but impotent to do anything to protect her.

Had Cecelia found support from her siblings, the home situation might have been tolerable. But they generally sided with Dad; they didn't have the courage to stand up to him, or maybe they agreed with him. She didn't know. They didn't reveal beliefs so intimate as a political viewpoint. In any case, Cecelia felt separate from them all, and relatively unwelcome, every time she ventured home.

Fortunately, (and I think not coincidentally) she met a woman in a nursing class who experienced life with her family similarly. Her new acquaintance had gone to a twelve-step meeting for support and solace because her family was fraught with alcoholism. As Cecelia began to talk about her own home life—the first time she had ever openly done so—Abby suggested she come along to a meeting.

....

To surrender a position, a person, an opinion will change your life profoundly.

....

The way Cecelia explained it, her first visit was the very first time she felt even a ray of hope for how to survive in her family of origin. She didn't want to write them off. She loved them, after all, even though the pain was great. She had met many students who had made the choice to write their families off, but she knew she owed her very life to her family. She had always been well taken care of as far as her physical needs were concerned. Her father had a profitable business. She simply knew she couldn't live by their rules and hold her own head high. She wanted to learn how to navigate through the visits.

Cecelia's first twelve-step meeting, much like my own first meeting, was nothing like she had expected. She went seeking help to change her family, particularly her dad, and discovered the only help offered was suggestions for letting them be who they were while rejoicing in who she, herself, was. Cecelia was befuddled. Abby had told her to expect help. Freedom. She didn't consider what she heard much of either, and yet, she saw a ray of hope because the group was laughing about situations not unlike her own. She hadn't ever laughed about her family experiences.

Cecelia's perspective began to change as a result of the meetings she attended. She realized she could get free from her attachment to what her parents chose to believe. She didn't share their beliefs, and hadn't for years, but she also didn't want to react to it anymore. She wanted to freely love her dad, her mom and her siblings. The idea that she need not be unduly affected by them, regardless of their politics or personal philosophies, was a gift, one she began to cherish fully.

By the time of our conversation, she had been able to transfer what she had learned to do with her family to the other individuals in her life. Interestingly, her significant other shared many of the beliefs her family held. We laughed over this when she talked about it, and decided that perhaps the work she had done around the family issues was to prepare her for further practice with the man she had chosen to love.

Surrendering allows us to enjoy another's company, while avoiding the unnecessary conflicts. If we want to experience peace, we can decide that all conflicts are unnecessary.

I've said before on many occasions that we come here to learn certain lessons. And those we sit among are our teachers. Because I believe this, I also accept that my friends, my family, and my spouse are my constant teachers. And if the lesson I need to learn is "letting go," allowing others to be who they are, I will get myriad opportunities to surrender my attempts to control anyone else. Again and again, our teachers will appear and we will get our chance to practice, to hone to near perfection, the gift of surrendering. As we practice surrender, our life becomes more functional.

I met Bill only recently, but discovered pretty quickly that his own upbringing was far from healthy. He, like so many of us, wanted to find greater peace and joy in life. He was tired, he said. Tired of always fighting with others but winning no battles. He couldn't initially fathom the idea of surrendering to anything or anybody that he didn't respect—generally those with differing outlooks. He was pretty sure of himself and his opinions. He had been raised by a dad who was domineering so he "wore" that trait too. It didn't bring him joy, however. His wife and son rebelled and continued to do whatever they wanted. In this case, it was to abuse alcohol and pills.

I met Bill at a party, and because he dared to share a bit about his life and his struggles (certainly an unexpected revelation) I, in turn, shared what I had painstakingly learned about letting others have their own journey. I understood his dilemma all too well. My life had mirrored his in my first marriage and in many subsequent relationships. I had been adamant that others needed to change. And I was sure there was a convincing argument for getting them to change, but I had just not formulated it yet. I look back on this time in my life with embarrassment. I was a screecher. I was sure if I hollered loud enough I would get my point across. All I accomplished were failed relationships. No one wants to be controlled, demeaned, or ridiculed. I was a master at trying all three.

I was able to listen to Bill and relate to his story, and this gave him hope that change might happen for him in time, just as it had happened for me. I wasn't sure in that initial meeting that he truly understood that he couldn't change anyone unless they wanted to change. But he did give the twelve-step rooms a try at my suggestion. I saw him there a number of times and was amazed at how he seemed to be soaking up the wisdom that gets so freely expressed there.

As is so often said, when the student is ready, the teacher appears. Bill was ready and I crossed his path at just the right time. There are no coincidences. The rest may well be history if he continues to strengthen his options at seeing life, his wife, and his son from a different perspective. We can only change ourselves. But the miracle that so often occurs is that when we change, so do they.

....

Surrendering allows our fellow travelers to make their own mistakes, have their own successes, and determine their own journeys.

....

I find myself extremely moved by the very idea of surrender, no doubt because it has so changed my perspective, my level of peace, on a daily basis. I used to be that person who always wanted to tweak, even a tiny bit, "your" behavior, "your" opinion, "your" attire. I didn't know how to leave you alone. My own inner turmoil cried out for my outer world to change so that I'd feel safe. There is no safety in trying to change others. None whatsoever. There is only heartache and rejection.

Every day now I can look around myself and be glad that I have not a whit of power to change anyone else. The very act of trying to change others is exhausting. I can honestly celebrate the choices my husband and others make. I can love him and them so much more easily. Attending to one life—mine—rather than all the lives of the many who people my world is freedom. Surrender is the action. Freedom is the gift.

Let's look at one more example of the fruits of surrender. I have to talk about her because she is a treasure trove of wisdom. Her name is Nettie. Nettie has celebrated forty years in recovery. Exactly half her life. And to hear her tell it she came into the twelve-step rooms desperate, kicking, and screaming. She was angry that her husband was an alcoholic. Angry that he was unavailable as a parent. Angry that she felt tied to him because of her religious beliefs. And even angrier that she couldn't convince him that he was ruining their lives. She even imagined killing him, she said. I understood that. I had shared that fantasy about my first husband too, although I preferred that he'd simply die in an accident while driving drunk.

Surrendering releases us from all tension. It also changes the atmosphere in the home or workplace.

She came to her first meeting expecting nothing, she said. But she noted, from across the room, another woman close in age who wore a serene look on her face. Nettie longed to feel that way. She went up to the woman after the meeting and asked her how it was that she could be so serene. The woman said simply, "I gave up the battle." Nettie said she walked away knowing she wanted what that woman had. She also decided she was going to stick with this program. It was the first hope she had felt for more than fifteen years.

I want to tell you more about Nettie because her transformation has contributed to the transformation of so many others, too. She told me that the first thing she really absorbed was that every journey is unique and can't be changed by an outsider. In other words, she didn't have the power to effect a change in her husband. Her new friends said, "just let him be." This seemed unfathomable. She got a sponsor, a mentor who helped her understand the finer points of how the program suggestions worked. Fortunately she chose a woman whose home life resembled her own.

Helen told Nettie exactly how she survived in her family. She invited Nettie to try it her way. She never looked back. From that day forward she did what Helen told her; she let her husband be. He didn't really change his drinking, but Nettie's decision to let him be eased the tension in the house immeasurably. They remained together until he died, and she never again wished him dead. She just went about her own life and smiled a lot. He did likewise.

Every one of us who makes the choice to surrender, allowing the others on our path to chart their own course, is adding benefit to the entire human community.

Nettie told so many stories in the meetings we both attended. And every one of them stressed the miracle of surrender. She convinced us all that it was worth trying. Worth practicing. Worth perfecting, if anything can be perfected. I know that knowing Nettie has added to my joy. What she shared, I practiced. And I'm the better for it. So are my relationships. One of her best stories—it's an image, really—was of a limousine. She learned to let God be the driver, and she climbed into the back seat every day. That image gave me what I needed to focus on in those trying times, the times I was trying to be the driver of the limousine that carried everyone else who was important to me.

Surrendering allows us to enjoy the ride, our own and others'.

Before we look at the next great gift gained from a less than great upbringing, let's review what can be gained from the practice of surrendering and how the experiences of Cecelia, Bill, Nettie, and I can make a difference in how tomorrow can be lived. The wisdom of the others we all met in the twelve-step rooms moved us forward. The following reminders will move you forward too:

To surrender means to let go—to release from your control.

Surrendering allows our fellow travelers to make their own mistakes, have their own successes, and determine their own journeys.

Surrendering invites the God of our understanding to be the driver of our limousine.

It allows us to enjoy the ride, our own and others'.

Surrendering allows us to enjoy another's company, avoiding the unnecessary conflicts. All conflicts are unnecessary.

Surrendering releases us from all tension. It also changes the atmosphere in the home or workplace.

Surrendering sustains hope and fills every day with potential for good.

It is absolutely the greatest offering of respect we can give to friends, lovers, even strangers.

Surrendering does have a universal impact. It knows no bounds.

To surrender a position, a person, or an opinion will change your life completely, and for all time.

Every one of us who makes the choice to surrender, allowing the others on our path to chart their own lives, is adding benefit to the entire human community. Is this a benefit you want to share in? The choice is now.

Further Reflection

Before leaving this chapter, give yourself a few more minutes to digest what you have read here. Do you see, now, where and when you surrendered a position recently? Can you see where you resisted and kept growth from occurring, yours and someone else's? Consider writing a few thoughts in response to these questions. Share where you are with this concept with someone you trust. Now ask yourself, "Am I committed to making surrender a daily practice?"

6

Healing through Connection and the Power of Oneness

Humankind has not woven the web of life. We are but one thread within it. Whatever we do to the web, we do to ourselves. All things are bound together. All things connect.

Chief Seattle

We must connect with others if we are to heal. We must.

It is mind-bending, particularly to the uninitiated, to comprehend that all members of the human community, in fact all life forms, are connected in a most sacred way, just as surely as all the threads in a tapestry are woven into a unique and beautiful design. When we fully absorb this fact it's also spiritually satisfying, because it assures us that we are not dangling all alone in this universe, hanging by a thin thread that can break at any moment. Indeed, we are not dangling at all. We are connected.

I didn't feel any sense of connection, of being joined to any other person or to anything in the natural world, prior to taking my seat in the twelve-step rooms. And my awareness of connection didn't happen right away. As a matter of fact, even though I generally felt it while sitting in a meeting, it was gone once I got home to my empty apartment. Alone, I was haunted by the feeling of "dangling alone in the universe" once again.

My family of origin didn't comfort me with the connection all humans crave, but not because they made a conscious choice to be disconnected from me. They simply didn't know how to do something they had not experienced themselves. Nor did I get that craving genuinely satisfied through alcohol, drugs, and the many people I claimed as my hostages prior to turning my life over to the God of my new understanding. My search for connection had taken insidious forms. The perpetual unease I felt was debilitating. And my drive to relieve it, from age thirteen on, nearly destroyed me. I heard the same story from so many other people.

My drugs of choice gave me only intermittent relief from the isolation I felt. I don't think I understood at the time what was happening. I surely didn't know I was becoming dependent on alcohol or men for my wavering sense of well-being, but both were temporarily providing it, nonetheless. Gravitating to the opposite sex for attention felt so natural. Unfortunately men didn't really protect me from the haunting isolation I felt. In my misguided search for connection, I was traveling at a high rate of speed down a dead end street.

Sitting here today, telling this story, convinces me of the ever-present constant of God in my life. This constant is in your life, too. There is no other explanation for the fact that I survived to tell my story and to gather the stories of others to share with you. And that you have survived to read them. The connection we crave, you and I, has always been "a fact of our existence." Our fearful ego just prevented us from feeling it.

It's key to remember that we are, in reality, always connected. We simply don't recognize it.

I now know that I was never disconnected from God's loving attention, nor was it possible for me to be separate from all other life forms either. Our ego has unyielding power to keep us from being aware that we are forever safe and always just where we need to be, in contact with those we need to know, experiencing all that we agreed to experience. Now that I understand the divine nature of our journey, my soul is quieted.

I prefer to think of e-g-o as an acronym for **e**dging-**G**od-**o**ut. That way I always understand just what is really going on when I am in a state of mild depression. When I feel that sense of ennui, even today, I know that my ego has risen to assert control over my thoughts and feelings. I do wish I could say this doesn't happen to me anymore, but alas, I have to be vigilant or my ego will "act out" and I'll feel separate, alone, and very vulnerable—a place I do not relish.

I have just come through a period like this. I can't be certain what brought it on. Perhaps returning to our northern home after a winter in Florida triggered it. Or maybe the loss of another dear friend. In a period of fourteen months, five very good friends have passed away. Even though I fully believe in an afterlife, and all five of these friends made a transition that wasn't entirely unexpected, just knowing that I can never sit down and have a cup of coffee with any of them again makes me very sad. Three of the five were women I had known for more than twenty-five years, and we had shared thousands of hours of good times. I feel a hole in my heart just talking about this. But at the same time, talking about it is what will heal me and you, when there is that need. I also believe that my connection to them has continued, just in a different form. I consider them the "hovering angels" who watch over my every move. A wonderful image, and a special kind of joining.

The recognition of our connection to others is our path to healing, and yet, how easily overlooked this is. Without this recognition we live very much in our unease and isolation, and this is deadly. That deadening of the soul is what draws so many of us to the poor choices that often bring us close to death. That I escaped the many dark alleys and dangerous liaisons owes solely to the God of my understanding who had never relinquished His hold on me, a hold of which I wasn't even conscious.

One of the biggest tragedies of dysfunctional families is that most family members actually live unaware of their isolation from one another. It's not that they don't feel the separation, but they just don't have words for it. Most tragic of all, they don't understand that it could be different. They don't know that there is a solution to the loneliness they feel, or that the solution is to reach out to one another, to truly *see* each other. But when no one has offered that hand to you, or revealed his or her own vulnerability, the door to the openness that heals remains closed.

....

Our isolation from others contributed to our dysfunction,
both in the family and separate from the family.

....

Letting others know exactly how we feel, even in our brokenness, is the invitation that leads to wholeness—theirs as well as ours. And when any two people consciously make a connection, or recognize one that has always been there, a shift in the universe occurs. We are waking up, recognizing what always has been—the web of life.

How grateful I am that for the last nearly forty years I have been privy to the knowledge of God's presence in my life and the connection to the universe that is the gift we all share. When I forget His presence and the connection it assures us, the old fears that governed my life before regain control.

How fortunate, especially in these moments of forgetting, to be journeying with men and women who understand the truth, even if they don't always remember it. It's not an accident that this is so. As I've already mentioned, our journey is divine, our path is predetermined, and we selected our own encounters a long time ago. We share the assignment to serve as teachers as well as students within our many connections.

It intrigues me and has for years that many of us have had to experience the overwhelming ennui of imagined *disconnection* in order to finally seek, and to really feel, what was always true: *connection!* It's a mind bender to become aware, however that happens, of the reality of who we are and have always been in the living universe, in spite of our denial of this awareness. Among the many I interviewed for this book, no one claimed more certainty in early life that he traveled alone, needing no one in his life, than Charlie, the pilot. He had been a very proud loner, he said. As mentioned in an earlier chapter, he had many siblings, all girls, and he had never planned to marry. He didn't want to need someone or be needed either. His vocation made it easy to "fly solo" through life. He was sure it had made him an attractive catch too, which made his conquests of women all the more exciting and successful.

The unexpected did happen, however. He found his way into twelve-step rooms and discovered, as so many do, that life has much more to offer than heretofore expected. Forging connections to similarly minded travelers began to interest him. In his family of origin, the warmth of connection didn't exist because there were too many people going in too many directions, and alcohol masked whatever desire for connection might have existed. It became natural to seek isolation rather than dare to be vulnerable, which could be taken advantage of. That expectation is what we commonly imagine will happen with strangers too, so when Charlie first came into "the rooms," he maintained his distance for safety reasons, he said.

Connection can begin in the simplest of ways.

What Charlie felt the first time he held hands in the closing prayer was the warmth of connection, however, and it took him by surprise. He said he felt "a presence," and didn't know what it meant, only that he wanted to feel it again. Because of our unease we fear the very antidote until it happens, even against our will at first. And then we seek it again and again, much like we sought the effects of our alcohol or drug consumption. Both elevate us. Both change our perspective. Both give us hope. But just one of them offers hope that heals.

Charlie did heal. And he nurtured his connections to many others. He began with his family, some of whom chose the same path he had selected. He sought the connection with newfound friends. Eventually he even considered sharing his life, full-time, with a woman he met in the rooms. She understood the importance of connection, he said. She was a walking example of it, in fact. He said the risk of letting her know him fully, which is truly necessary if disconnection and isolation are to be healed, lessened, and he took the plunge.

Now, many years later, Charlie and this woman continue to walk the walk and share the path of connection, serving as an example to many others that vulnerability is worth the risk for the payoff it promises.

There were a number of interviewees whose lives now reflected a very different worldview than the one they had nurtured for decades. My role with each of them was so intimate, really. Having others reveal who they were, what happened, and who they are now was like experiencing a speaker's meeting over and over again. And in every instance, what had been a downward spiraling life became an example of miraculous survival and an example to others that nothing has to defeat us. There is no dysfunction too great to be lessened and then healed if we are willing to close the separation that has existed for so long between us.

....

Unless we vulnerably connect with others we cannot heal our ailing souls.

....

William is a superb example of this. You remember William—he had a cold, neurotic mother, an unavailable, older sister, and a father who strictly maintained his distance from the family whenever possible. Thus the family consisted of four individuals who rarely spoke to one another; when conversation did occur, it was curt, oftentimes demeaning, and never loving or joyful. William, as you will recall, excelled in sports so that he'd have something he could point to with pride, but his parents never acknowledged his pursuits. They never attended his games. They never followed his activities at all.

William did make friends relatively easily, owing to his excellence as an athlete and student. But, like Charlie, he didn't allow himself to connect with anyone at an emotional level. It was safer that way. He was also very lonely, but that was a feeling he was comfortable with. He let down his guard when he married the first time, but as you might recall, his wife died a long, slow death from cancer. William's vulnerability was bruised, for sure. And by the time of his second marriage, he had steeled himself to remain relatively aloof. Even when his wife's alcoholism became apparent to some, he tried to ignore it; that is, until it interfered with her role as mother.

William's wife had been sober on and off so he could ignore her disease. It was an illness he didn't even believe in initially, until it spilled over into their family life all too often. Then it became time for action and he turned to Al-Anon, took his seat, and soaked up the good news about connection and how it heals us. No dysfunction is sacrosanct. All of them give way to connection, eventually, a connection that quietly mends the ailing heart.

Healing is the reason for being among one another. Our tasks are to witness and listen and nurture.

What is it about connection that is so special, that changes us so completely? All of my years in the twelve-step rooms of recovery, which have included literally thousands of meetings, thus tens of thousands of individual encounters with people, have convinced me that looking into the eyes of someone else, offering them rapt attention, and being a witness to their story is what expands one's heart. By doing all these things, we in turn invite the healing to happen. We don't heal alone. We heal in concert with others. William began to heal, he said, from the very first meeting he attended. He had never heard others talk so openly or vulnerably about their struggles, struggles he too had experienced in his life, particularly in his family of origin. He knew he had gone to the right place for help.

When I met William, I could sense he was accessible, a soul seeking healing. I could immediately connect because of his openness to and sharing the wisdom he had already gathered. And because I sometimes sat in the same meetings, I could observe how eager he was to include others in the good news he had discovered. He set such a good example and could draw others along so easily because he spoke with such clarity and conviction. He had suffered. For years he had suffered, alone and lonely, but now he was healing and he wanted others to see that they could heal too. He was one of the first people in the circle at the end of every meeting to offer a hug and a kind word to newcomers and old timers alike. He had become the embodiment of connection before my very eyes.

Connection requires vulnerability. It also blesses those who share.

It doesn't happen that way or that quickly for everyone who longs to feel the connection that William felt. Valerie, for one, remains rather guarded. Although her story makes it apparent that she has come a long way, she has had a long way to come. Her family of origin, if you'll remember, was extremely damaging to her psyche. Her father died with nothing resolved, and her mother, though finally sober and in contact with Valerie, remains guarded herself. Valerie is slow to trust, and when trust is lacking, genuine connection is too. The obvious happens next: no trust, no connection, no sustained healing. Even though Valerie has worked hard to heal her wounds, they persist. Lucky for her she has a special someone in her life, and providing she reaches out and allows that person in, she gets a daily reprieve.

When I think about my own healing as a result of the connections I have made and continue to make daily, I am convinced that no one has to live a wounded life unless they choose to. The tiniest of connections is a beginning. What are some of these? Smiling at a stranger. Asking the clerk at the grocery if she or he has had a good day. Calling a friend or relative just to let them know you are thinking of them. Taking a few minutes to meditate in order to secure your own connection with the God of your understanding. Making a point of ending the day with a prayer of thanksgiving. We have to do our part in the connecting process if we want to change how we experience the events of the day.

....

Smiles, soft expressions, quiet questions, kind responses, prayers, and meditation are just a very few of the techniques for connecting.

....

One of the people I spoke with who connected in an almost mystical way with others was Harry. What made this so surprising from my perspective was that of all the people I interviewed, his family of origin might well have been the most dysfunctional. His brother was certifiably mentally ill, both parents were unavailable in their own way, and out of desperation, he turned to heavy drugs in his junior high years. Heroin was his drug of choice, and until the day he got clean he never gave any thought to really changing the way he navigated through life. He expected to be dead by age thirty.

I met Harry early on in my own recovery and was stunned by how easily he shared his emotions, how quickly he identified them and, in the process, made it acceptable for those listening to him to be vulnerable too. I believe the first time I talked to him, he cried. And he cried often as he listened to others share too. I have actually been more than occasionally in contact with Harry for many years and have been able to observe his healing both from afar and through the many conversations we have had. I am inclined to say that he actually embodies connection at a deeper level than ordinary human beings. When you converse with Harry, his attention to your words is intense. His questions are piercing and intimate, not out of nosiness but because he genuinely cares, unlike so many who engage us in conversation.

In my observation, one way that Harry affects change in others is through the unmistakable way he zeroes in on your struggle, whatever it is. He can mind-read, it seems. Lives change because of Harry.

....

Without conscious connection, no healing will occur.

....

We make tiny changes in how we take notice of those we travel among, creating threads of connection that forge deeper bonds. We are alive in this moment in time to experience the healing that results from these bonds. What a thrill it has been for me to talk to so many and learn how connection manifests itself, bringing about a changed human being, a changed family, a changed community, and finally a changed universe. It reminds me of what Mother Teresa said so many years ago: "Be kind to every one. And start with the person standing next to you." What we do for one, we do for all. What we take from one, we take from all. The question we have to confront is, "Am I adding to the goodness, the connection of the human community, or am I detracting from it?" Whatever the answer, we can address it accordingly.

The gifts we gather from surviving our dysfunctional families are adding up, as you can see. We can claim resilience, perseverance, a sense of humor, the ability to embrace forgiveness as well as surrender, and now the ability to truly connect to the journeys of others in an intimate way. Our growth has been phenomenal. We need to be proud of our hard work. Survival is, in and of itself, a feather in one's cap. To get to claim all of these gifts stands for so much more beyond mere survival.

Before we turn our attention to the next big gift, let's review what we learned about connection from these few stories:

Our isolation from others contributed to our dysfunction, both in the family and separate from the family.

Unless we vulnerably connect with others we cannot heal our ailing souls.

Connection can begin in the simplest of ways.

Smiles, soft expressions, quiet questions, kind responses, prayers, and meditation are just a very few of the techniques for connecting.

It's key to remember that we are, in reality, actually already connected. We simply don't recognize it.

To now recognize it makes the conscious act of connecting easier.

Connection is always happening with more than two. Any single connection is really making a connection with everyone.

Connection is akin to the waves in the ocean. They never stop in the forward momentum that brings them to the shore.

Connection requires vulnerability. It also blesses those who share.

Without conscious connection, no healing will occur.

Healing is the reason for being among one another. Our tasks are to witness and listen and nurture.

Further Reflection

Before closing this chapter, let's consider some examples of recent connections we have made with loved ones or strangers. Share them here or elsewhere.

What healing has yet to be initiated in your life? Can you conceive of a plan for beginning the process?

What connections have you made that have impacted you the most? Why these?

7

Discerning Real Love

Being deeply loved by someone gives you strength, while loving someone deeply gives you courage.

Lao Tzu

Strength and courage. What great ways to describe how love can manifest.

To love deeply and fully creates both the connection we crave and the freedom we need, neither of which most of us had growing up in our dysfunctional families. For the most part we felt neither a sense of meaningful connection nor free from the family's expectations, and their oftentimes unhealthy hold on us. But we are gathering new tools now; we are learning a new way to perceive the world around us, and in the process we are learning that real love doesn't permit us to hold someone hostage. Nor does it mean we will be taken hostage ourselves. We free others to live, to fly away if that's their journey. And we fly free as well. The grand reward of real love is real growth for all of us.

Unfortunately, love is a word that is too often used frivolously. As a case in point, how often do you say, "Love you," when saying goodbye to someone on the phone, or leaving the company of even a casual friend following lunch or a walk? Perhaps it is someone you actually do love; however, it becomes a "throwaway" comment in many instances, lacking real meaning, quite often not conveying sincerely honest feelings.

I don't mean to suggest that we shouldn't freely express love—we should. But I do think it's wise to consider what we mean by the term and perhaps be more selective about using it so that it retains more meaning, for us and for the recipient. Please don't misunderstand: behaving in a loving way is *always kind, always good, and always healing.* Some spiritual pathways I'm familiar with, *A Course in Miracles* specifically, propose that *all* expressions made by any of us fall into one of two categories: *love or fear.* Even so, saying "I love you" at random moments isn't necessarily honest, is it? Don't we sometimes wonder if the person expressing it really means it? Doesn't it even seem a bit manipulative at times? Perhaps it's manipulation that is rooted in fear.

We are learning how to respond to love and recognize fear.

Let's consider that the confusion about love and its meaning might be the result of growing up in families where love was often expressed conditionally. "If you do this, then I will love you more." I always felt that in order to be loved by my family of origin, certain conditions had to be met. And if those conditions weren't met, shame was used quite freely—for not performing well in school or in other extracurricular activities. Knowing an expectation was always being placed on me made achievement more difficult. In my case, it made rebellion more appealing too.

Perhaps not all families lay conditions on their offspring, but I'm inclined to think that most dysfunctional families do. The primary condition for receiving the desired love is to attain a certain expected level of performance. Always. When Charlie asked why he didn't get paid like other kids did for good quarterly grades, his mother's response was always the same: "I *expect* you to get all A's." An environment of high expectations and scant praise was a common refrain for many I spoke to.

Perhaps it's the generation many of my interviewees are part of. After all, the parents of many of them are quite elderly now, in some cases even dead. Growing up in a very different era made those parents far less concerned about stroking the egos of their children. They survived the difficulties of WWII, the Korean Conflict, and the Depression Years, which gave them a very different perspective on life. Life was hard, even tragic, for many of them. Thus they saw no reason to make the load for their children extremely light. Hard work paid dividends. That's how they saw it. That's what their experience had shown them.

It wasn't that they didn't love their children; of course they did, but expressing it wasn't all that comfortable. Setting a good example for hard work was easier. I remember pretty seriously doubting my parents' love. For certain, I have no recollection of them *ever* saying "I love you" when I was young—not to me or my siblings, and not to each other. Overt signs of their love simply weren't apparent. Anger, on the other hand, was observed almost daily.

And at some point I began to think that, just maybe, I had been adopted (I suppose due to my parents' lack of expressed love and my overactive imagination). To prove my point, I occasionally played an insidious game of "remember when" to see if I could catch them being totally unaware of a certain incident that I knew had happened in our family, quite possibly with those "other parents I was sure were mine." What an insane idea I harbored in my childhood. Surprisingly, some others I spoke with had suspected the same thing. Perhaps this is common with all children whose home life is tense. For sure, mine was tension-filled nearly every day.

We will always recognize love if given enough time.

Love is oftentimes vague, unclear, or nebulous. That's one of the things my interviews revealed. And then when it's unspoken, doubt is triggered in the minds of those who are seeking assurance about their worth, regardless of age. When the die has been cast in childhood, its roots are deep and not easily dislodged. I can recount examples from every interviewee's life that reflect this kind of doubt. William comes to mind immediately. His parents didn't express anything like loving kindness to him or his sister when they were young. Both parents were very cold and aloof, toward each other as well as toward the children. Pretty typical for Scandinavians, some might say. Feeling quite separate and alone didn't seem unusual to William until he became friends with his first wife. Her family was far different from his own—she had four siblings and a jovial set of parents. They welcomed William in with open arms.

It wasn't easy for William to be as open and expressive as Anna was, initially, but his desire to be so, coupled with his perseverance and her patience, allowed him to develop that skill and to be, in time, far more loving than either of his parents had any notion of being. Anna's death eight years into their marriage, an eight-year journey that was consumed by her cancer, was a real tragedy. William withdrew from others, becoming once again protected, separate, and distant just like his parents had been, to prevent himself from being vulnerable and open to hurt again. That's how he remained well into his second marriage, even though he fathered two children. He wanted them to feel his love and he showed it in many ways, but expressing it in words was hard.

For William, the really good news was that he longed for more. And the even better news was that he finally found it—in a most unlikely place, as far as he was concerned. Among strangers! That's who we are to one another when we wander into the twelve-step rooms. Utter strangers become sincerely loving friends—friends who seldom even know each other's last names. From one other we learn what love looks like. We learn how to accept it. How to express it. How to savor it. We also learn why we were not able to recognize it or offer it either. It's a learning curve for all of us, but lives change. One by one we help each other claim a new perspective and live a new experience.

....

Conditional love isn't love at all. Do you give love fully and freely?

....

William is a great discerner of love now, and he is willing to express it. What we learn in "the rooms" is that we must give away that which we want to keep. William is a great example to all of us. He is the first one to welcome the newcomer and the one who is always quick to share how his life has moved from isolation to inclusion, which he never imagined before crawling into the rooms of Al-Anon.

Although I observed Nettie, the woman with forty years in Al-Anon, fewer times than I did William, I was able to see that she, too, gave love freely and expected nothing in return. She had been helped so much by the twelve steps that she made a point of saying she stayed active even after forty years of attendance because of her commitment to give back. That's love in spades! And everyone felt it. She didn't seek a bargain. She wanted others to receive what she had been so freely given. There were no conditions. Real love never has conditions. It joins two or more together and the bond is simply felt, with or without being verbally acknowledged.

The more I explore love, the more I can comfortably say that true love is *total*. It is full acceptance. It is making a space for the feelings of others and embracing what is, and it is joining with someone else where they are, not where I think they ought to be.

We can always discern when we are in the presence of a loving person. We feel free to be ourselves. There is no judgment. An unspoken joy can be detected. Fortunately we learn by example. No one I spoke to felt fully loved as a child. No one recalled their family as supporting them wholly, loving them completely, or accepting everything about them—their opinions, their actions, their dreams.

We wouldn't very likely have ended up in the rooms where I found my interview subjects had we already felt the way we all sought to feel. The way most of us were/ are beginning to feel at last. I haven't introduced you to Marilee yet, but it's time. She embodies how everyone wants to feel. She is the expression of love personified. But she didn't used to be that way. She was scared and never spoke. She sat, withdrawn, even avoiding eye contact. She was the only one in her family who dared to seek help, but they all needed it, she said, at long last. Alcoholism was rampant in the family but no one was allowed to acknowledge it. It was the family secret. And then she moved away and timidly, at first, gave the twelve-step rooms a try.

When we talked, she said she initially doubted that anything could be of help. She survived so much damage in her family of origin. She came out of desperation and loneliness. Neither her husband nor her kids understood the depth of her despair. With nowhere to turn, she showed up and sat quietly for weeks, she said, just listening. She felt subtly loved and accepted but didn't know why. Little by little, she let others in. And the more she let them in, the more she absorbed. As she allowed herself to be loved, she too was able to love. Now, the first expression that comes from her lips is a loving one. No one is left outside of her expression, and it's genuine. The more she gives the more there is to give. We can all see it. Anyone who wants to discern real love only needs to observe Marilee. In a few short years she has become the person we all want to emulate. And she is willing to show us how she has done it. A smile. A hug. A sincerely loving expression and a prayer for your well-being. She is ready to give all of these to all of us every minute.

Marilee offers a sweeping acceptance to everyone who joins our circle of recovery. Her own healing is the direct result of helping others heal, she says. I don't doubt it. She has been a very quick study, much like William. As I said earlier, I have filled a chair in the rooms since 1974. And my growth has been slower, far slower. Did I resist? Perhaps. I didn't really understand the process of turning my life and will over to the care of a loving God. I had never had a relationship with Him. I was doubtful that I needed one. Fortunately, I stuck around long enough to see the benefits others were claiming. I wanted them too.

The recognition of love—learning how to accept it along with expressing it—has given my life the richness that gets me up every day. Adding this benefit to all of the others that have come to me and the people in these pages might, I hope, convince you that the gifts we can claim from our dysfunctional family of origin far outweigh the stumbling blocks. Having both provides the contrast that truly informs us, now and in the future.

We have met our teachers everywhere.

There is one more person I simply must introduce you to before moving to the next chapter. Her name is Helene. She came from a family of thirteen. To hear her describe it, Mom was always way too busy mothering little kids or praying about the safety of the acting-out older ones to pay much attention to Helene and the other siblings who were in the middle. Like so many of us who grew up in families with multiple children, she had no idea if she was on her mother's radar screen. For sure she knew she wasn't on her dad's. As a consequence, she began acting out while in grade school and the nuns were quick to punish her, pointing out that she was not headed for Heaven, where her siblings were headed.

She hated the incessant comparisons, but they continued, which triggered more acting out, and at the age of fifteen she ran away for the first time. She wanted to make her family feel bad. She wanted them to apologize to her for ignoring her. She didn't get that result. Nor did she get the assurance of love that she craved. Like me and so many others, she began to search for love in all the wrong places and had no idea how to discern the real thing.

Helene did find her way to some solution for her troubled journey. We are all traveling a chosen path. That's the beauty of understanding that the journey is divine. *We will eventually get to where we need to be when the time is right.* We just don't know that while in the midst of our haunting fear.

....

We know now that fear can be relinquished with a decision.

....

As mentioned earlier in this chapter, and in my other books too, we live from a place of fear or love. One or the other has completely commandeered our mind. Growing up in dysfunctional families pretty much guarantees that fear has held us hostage. Learning, as we eventually do while sitting in twelve-step rooms, that we can shift our perspective and relinquish our fear, offers us a clear indication of hope. Hope then leads to love. Hope opens our hearts to see anew. Hope changes everything about the present moment and all future moments too. Nothing changes if nothing changes. And everything changes when we replace fear with hope, which carries us quickly to love, and all that love promises us. Love's many gifts are unending.

Nothing releases us into love but our own willingness to move forward, our own willingness to make a new decision, our own willingness to let God be in charge. Love is a constant in our lives, whether we are aware of it or not. God has been a constant too. He has never held back, even if we didn't acknowledge receiving His love. But how do we really know this to be the case? Let's recount some of the ordinary experiences that prove it:

We are alive now, reading these words.

We have met our teachers everywhere.

We have learned how to respond to love.

We will always recognize love if given enough time.

We know now that fear can be relinquished with a decision.

Because we put our differences aside when we love one another, we benefit the world around us too.

What we do to one, we do to all. Love works the same way if it's true love.

Conditional love isn't love at all. Do you give love fully and freely?

There are many ways to describe love: acceptance, joining with, fully embracing, supportive emotionally, walking alongside of, witnessing to. How many of these are you practiced at?

Further Reflection

Ask yourself, "Am I showing up the way I want to in all of my relationships?" And if you are not, if you express more fear than love, for instance, take some time to think about how you want to redirect your responses to those people you walk among. Remember, they are there by divine appointment.

8

Embracing the Strength of Kindness

*Three things in human life are important. The first is to
be kind. The second is to be kind. The third is to be kind.*

Henry James

There is no mystery in describing kindness. We all
recognize it. We all know when we have expressed
it. And we know when we have been showered with
kindness. It feels good, whichever side of kindness we
live on in the moment.

The decision to be kind is both ordinary and extraordinary, simultaneously. Kindness is ordinary in its simplicity, but quite extraordinary in its power to change
people, and therefore relationships, communities, work-
places, and ultimately the world. Most often, kindness
is a single tiny gesture—perhaps only a nod of the head
or the mere hint of a smile. Occasionally it's huge—an
unexpected visit from a loved one who lives on the other
side of the country, for instance. Or a bouquet of roses
from a secret admirer. Perhaps a note from a loved one, a

simple note that says, "I am thinking of you." Kindness is expressed in as many ways as the human mind can imagine. No one of them is preferable. They all count equally, particularly to one who has been bruised by life.

Kindness is most easily explained as an attitude, and clearly, we are always in control of our attitude. It's one of the few things that are never out of our control, as a matter of fact. Obviously, that means we can constantly be kind. But are we? The answer is no. We'd far prefer to blame others for the lousy attitude we have some days. "If only he hadn't done this or said that, I'd be okay," for instance. The excuses we manufacture for our negative state of mind are many, and pointless, and they infect the world around us. Let's not forget that we are one. We are interconnected; what touches you touches me in time too.

As said before, I am deeply moved by the words of Mother Teresa, who said: "Be kind to everyone and start with the person standing next to you." The impact we can have on the world we share, if we choose to be kind in every circumstance or even in an occasional situation, simply can't be overestimated. The shift in how life would feel to everyone is truly beyond description. This may seem far-fetched, but if we remember the butterfly effect from chaos theory, the impact I'm talking about will be obvious. *Anything that happens in one place is felt every place in due time. Anything. Everything.*

....

Kindness adds benefit to the lives of every one alive.

....

Because this is true—indisputable, in fact—never refuse to be kind. Never. That doesn't mean you have to let others take advantage of you. It only means that in your exchanges, your encounters with friends as well as strangers, you always respond pleasantly. Gently. It eases your life to make this decision. And it gives you a sense of healthy empowerment. If we respond negatively to someone who has been unkind to us, we have given them power over us. Some say we have given them "rent-free space in our minds." Snarling at someone may feel justified for a moment, even good, but the positive feeling doesn't last. In fact, it leaves very quickly.

I think of myself as a kind person now, at least most of the time; in my youth and even in the early years of my recovery, I was often on the lookout for a trade-off. What could I get in return for my kindness to you? In those days my kindness fell into the category of codependence. I tried to "buy favors" by being kind. If I went out of my way to please you, maybe you wouldn't abandon me. Alas, it never worked. When you grow up in a dysfunctional family, it's common to bargain in that way.

We walk a fine line, though, when it comes to kindness. If we honor Mother Teresa's words, and I try to, we are kind to everyone, no exceptions. But might this not look like manipulation, on occasion? That we are being kind only for a hoped-for result? Perhaps. However, we always know if we have a "hidden" motive for our kindness. If we do, we have negated kindness completely. True kindness is always given freely with no expectation in return.

Making the decision to be kind in every situation seems like a tall order, perhaps, but it also can simplify one's life. When I make that choice, and as I've already said, I sincerely try to make it every day, the hours pass so much more smoothly. My interactions are fruitful and I know that I am showing up in the world in a way that pleases God, that fulfills His will for me. There is a great line from *A Course in Miracles* that I'll paraphrase here: "If the thought I am thinking or the action I am contemplating wouldn't please God, exchange it for one that would." This bit of simple guidance is mind-altering and day-changing.

Turning my life and my will over to God, the third step of the twelve I was introduced to in the rooms of the fellowship, didn't come easily at first. It seemed both unnecessary and way too risky. I know I made it too complicated—I expected God's will for me to be long on detail, and something I would dread doing. I didn't know how to listen to God, thus couldn't guess what His will was, so fortunately I read two books that proved to be extremely significant to my spiritual enlightenment: *The Magical Mystical Bear* by Matthew Fox, and a tiny little book by Brother Lawrence titled *The Practice of the Presence of God.* In both books I was assured that God's will was not mysterious, nor complicated. He was merely my companion, my friend who wanted to accompany me on my journey. In turning my life and my will over to God, I was only responsible for being kind.

....

Being kind is a choice we can make and remake throughout the day.

....

This awareness has changed my life. To smile, to offer a tiny prayer of gratitude or a prayer of hope on behalf of someone we know, or on occasion even a perfect stranger, is an act that shifts who we are and what we think of ourselves. It's an act that shifts the people around us too. We simply don't give enough credence to how connected we are through every action we take, even every thought we harbor. As has already been established, we are not wandering through life disconnected from one another. Not at all. What affects you likewise affects me. And there is true spiritual joy in that fact if you see it from the right perspective.

My own family of origin didn't look at life from this perspective. I honestly don't remember ever hearing a discussion about kindness at the supper table. Nor did I observe genuine acts of kindness on any regular basis between my parents, or between them and my siblings and me. I don't think their treatment of us was intentionally cool, dismissive, and distant. It just wasn't a family trait to be snuggly and kind, quick to give hugs or expressions of love. It was never their daily focus, and how sad that makes me feel, even to this day.

Eventually I did learn about kindness, and perhaps that's all that finally matters. We are born to learn certain lessons in life and sometimes we learn about things as the result of their absence in our most significant relationships. The key aspect here is that my learning about kindness meant I was able to act on it with the others who crossed my path as divinely directed.

Even though Janet's family didn't see life from a kind and loving perspective either, she *did* see it that way. She knew her actions affected others. Her entire upbringing had been complicated by the negative effects of her parents' behavior and her one brother's behavior. He had sexually molested her. The additional insult was that her parents never believed her, and never even asked him about it. Because of the trauma she lived with and had to overcome, she took special care with her own children. If they had a "story" to tell, she stopped what she was doing and listened. And she believed them. And she treated them with loving kindness, always.

We learn to honor others, to bless them with kindness, as the result of a host of experiences. One of Janet's most frequent remarks was "bless their hearts." Often I heard her say this in response to someone's unkind action or dismissive words. She gave blessings instead of criticism. For certain, she set an example for all of us. Even while going through a very acrimonious divorce, from a very vindictive, mentally unstable man, she spoke no unkind words. She knew, deep in her heart, where her words could take her, and she wanted to stay on the high road.

Remember that if others are not kind, they are hurting.

Choosing to remain on the high road is a good choice for all of us. And it's a great goal to strive for every day. We might even consider meditating about that image every morning for a few minutes as a reminder for how we want to experience the day. Many renowned individuals come to mind when I think about staying on that path. The Dalai Lama said, "Be kind whenever possible. It is always possible." Former President Jimmy Carter is considered by many to be an extremely kind man, as is Nelson Mandela. We don't have to focus on well-known people, however; perhaps a neighbor comes to mind, or a friend from childhood. The point is to consider what actions others have taken that put them in the category of kindness and then seek your own way to emulate them. My grandmother on my mother's side comes to mind. I strive to be like her.

When I think of the harsh realities of some people's lives and how they have chosen to be kind regardless, I know they are serving as examples to all of us that we never have to let the past injustices we survived determine our present actions. I referred to Mandela just a moment ago and he comes to mind as a man who was unjustly treated, to the extreme, but who lives from a place of loving kindness. And the Dalai Lama too. *Nothing that was ever done to us has to define who we are. We define ourselves.* Moment by moment.

No doubt many of you have read Viktor Frankl's *Man's Search for Meaning* about his experiences in a concentration camp. He had every good reason to be completely destroyed by his experiences, but he wasn't. The treatment was inhumane beyond one's imagination, but like other survivors who have shared their stories in memoirs, he refused to be conquered by the treatment that was inflicted on him. He understood at his very core the importance of defining one's self, of never letting how others treat you determine who you are.

....

Having lived through many unkind experiences doesn't have to define our lives today.

....

This is an attitude we must master if we are to wend our way through life with any positive intention or outcome. So many of the people I interviewed for this book did master the right attitude, and they experienced a life filled with hope and the rewards of their acts of kindness as the payoff.

I must now turn to Sheri. I first met Sheri because we had some friends in common. I immediately gravitated to her because of her laughter; she reminded me of a college friend. Like me, she was from the Midwest. I quickly learned how wise Sheri was when I went to a twelve-step meeting and heard her share a few words of wisdom. She had been "in the seats" for a long time. "Alcoholism is a family disease," she'd say at nearly every meeting. And then she'd share the pearls she had come to understand from being a regular attendee.

Sheri had been bruised by life, again and again, and yet you would never meet a kinder, more loving woman. She didn't believe in "payback." Nothing deterred her from kindness when she made up her mind to be kind. She said she had learned that every time she was kind, even in the face of ugly behavior from others, (and the ugliness had subsided very little with some members in her family), she felt empowered. She felt sure of herself. She felt hopeful and strong and determined.

The amazing thing about Sheri was that in spite of all the turmoil she lived with on a near daily basis, she always had a smile and a supportive gesture to make on behalf of others. She never failed to see the glass as half-full, even when the rest of us heard her stories and were convinced that "her" glass was half-empty. Sheri is a survivor. She is a role model. She is a constant mentor to others, whether in a formal or an informal way. We all watch her and know that living as she does will pay off in spades for us too.

Being kind is a choice we can make and remake throughout the day.

Kindness. It's all about kindness and the strength that comes from kindness. No one defines us without our consent. No one controls us without our consent. No one determines any one of our actions, opinions, ideas, or choices *without our consent*. If being kind is how we want to experience life and our fellow travelers, we will most likely meet kindness in return. And when we don't, we can remember that how others are isn't a reflection on us. How they are defines them. Period.

There is such freedom in choosing kindness as our persona. Just as with the other gifts discussed in the preceding chapters, we have developed into the great humans that we are by choice, by design, and by trust that God has always had our journey in His sights. What a lucky group of people we survivors are. Even though at some past time in our lives it appeared that all was lost, that we had been forsaken, now we know that God was present always. We also know that this will remain our truth for all time.

....

How we treat others shows them who we are.

....

Before moving into the next chapter I want to say a couple of things about Marilee again. I introduced you to her in the chapter on love because she embodies love so completely. Of course that means she embodies kindness too. Knowing her as I do from our many conversations, I would have to say that I find it unimaginable that Marilee could ever be unkind. She laughs and assures me otherwise, which reminds me that her kindness is a choice. She represents what kindness does for us, what it does also for the human community that gathers around us. She has a stillness about her that comforts without even having to express any specific words of kindness. She just is kindness, personified.

Was she always kind? Did she grow up in a house where she learned kindness? Absolutely not, she says. She did listen to her "guide," however, and everything that seemed to stand in her way rolled away as she practiced the "kindness tool." That's a good way to look at it, I think. You might recall that I referred to a similar idea from *A*

Course in Miracles that I paraphrased: *if you are thinking a thought or planning an action that wouldn't please God, let it go and choose one that would.* That small adjustment to our way of being in this world would change everything about our experience of living. It would change the experience of everyone else too. Everyone else!

The simplicity of this message is astounding. Our willingness to complicate it is equally astounding. *Just for today, let's practice kindness and take note of the quietly kind outcomes of all our experiences.* We just might make a decision about how to live that would make the rest of our lives truly peaceful. Let's begin by practicing the following:

Take a deep breath before responding in any situation.

Remember that if others are not kind, they are hurting.

Being kind is a choice we can make and remake throughout the day.

Having lived through many unkind experiences doesn't have to define our lives today.

Being kind doesn't require herculean effort. Try smiling.

Don't pick and choose whom you will be kind to. Be kind to everyone.

Make the decision to be kind and your life will suddenly feel more peaceful.

How we treat others shows them who we are.

Kindness invites respect from others.

Kindness adds benefit to the lives of everyone alive. Remember the butterfly effect.

Further Reflection

Before moving on, ask yourself, "Am I really practicing kindness in an honest way?" If you doubt this to be true, perhaps you can revisit some of the recent times you were less than kind or perhaps a bit manipulative with your kindness and "redo" them in your imagination. That way you can refrain from repeating old, bad habits.

9

Honoring Detachment as a Life-Giving Force

He who would be serene and pure needs but one thing, detachment.

Meister Eckhart

Detachment offers us the gift of freedom. No one can hold us hostage when we practice the "art" of detaching our emotions, and thus our reactions, from their behavior. Nor are we allowed to hold anyone else hostage. What a glorious way to live. Free. Unencumbered. Peaceful. Detachment can be practiced over and over until near perfection is achieved.

I was first introduced to the concept of detachment in a book by Jesuit Priest John Powell back in 1971. He didn't use the term "detachment" in his book, *Why Am I Afraid To Tell You Who I Am*, but from my perspective, that was the meaning behind a very compelling story he shared about a friend's reaction to a newspaper vendor. The vendor was typical "New York gruff" every morning. However, Powell's friend remained calm and even friendly, to the point of tipping the vendor on a regular basis when he strolled by to purchase his daily paper. "But why," John queried, "are you always nice to him? He is never anything but rude to you." His friend pleasantly responded, "Why should I let him decide what kind of day I am going to have?" Detachment personified!

At the time I read Powell's book, I had never been *unaffected* by anyone else's behavior. Never. My life was one big reaction to every person around me, even people I didn't know. It goes without saying that I had no serenity at all. Whatever you said or did, or didn't say or do, I reacted accordingly. I had no inner *guide*. Everyone acted as my guide, my value system, my "thinker," my controller. Thus I was always walking a tightrope. I tipped one way or the other depending on "you." Not having a life of my own didn't really even register on me. What a sad set of circumstances. I only knew that life felt pretty awful and that I was always "looking out there" to see how I should feel *in here*.

We can experience no peace of mind unless we let others go, to live their own lives.

Nothing changed for me for many years. Had I not developed severe addiction problems that led me into twelve-step programs, I may never have discovered that my primary "illness" was codependency, which is marked by extreme attachment and a clinginess that suffocated the "object" of my attention. My attachment was to anyone and everyone, including all of their behaviors. I was a master at reading what others were thinking so that I could respond accordingly. I craved approval. Not a healthy connection. I wanted to be on a pedestal—"his" pedestal. And whoever "he" might be was far less important than that there was *someone*. There was always someone. How dismal, yet how accurate this description is. Of course, alcohol became my constant companion, because it soothed my anxiety about impending rejection and my aching heart.

If I were the only person alive who lived this way it would be sad enough, but I met tons of people, particularly other women, who were similar in so many ways. We were seldom able to live from a place of inner direction, making choices that suited us rather than making choices we felt would suit our suitors. Fortunately for all the women I spoke with, something finally happened that changed all of that. It's my hope that what I share here about detachment can help women, and men too—that they can indeed make a different choice about how to live among their fellow travelers.

As already mentioned, it was 1971 when I first got a slight glimmering of what "detachment" was. But even when I went to my first Al-Anon meeting in 1974, I had no real understanding of the finer points of the term. I was still deeply entrenched in the moods, the behaviors, the opinions, and the actions of everyone who was within "screaming" distance of me. And I sought to learn how to control every one of those people and their myriad characteristics so that I could feel even a modicum of serenity in my own life. I was sure my request for help would be met with a "handbook" of sorts, which described exactly what I should do so that they would behave accordingly. This solution made perfect sense to me.

Detachment is freedom from relying on others to complete our lives.

The "old-timers" at the meeting provided an explanation of powerlessness and the role it was to play in my life. This was my first indication that going to Al-Anon wasn't offering the solution that I sought. In time I knew that it offered the *right* solution, however. It just made no sense to me at the beginning. Thank goodness I stuck around long enough *for the miracle to happen,* as we say in twelve-step recovery programs. For me the first miracle was sitting "at the feet," so to speak, of people who lived perfectly calm, peaceful lives even though the "qualifiers" in their lives were running amok in their disease of one "ism" or another. We might consider the blessing of powerlessness to be the first detachment theme.

I say the first theme of detachment because I think detachment wears many descriptions. I experience detachment in myriad ways: as freedom from obsession with others, as letting go of the journey of everyone but myself, as peacefully acknowledging my lack of control over everyone who walks beside me. Detachment has meant that no one's mood takes charge of my mood any longer, and that's a level of freedom I could not have imagined before embracing Al-Anon and the richness of its concepts, its principles, and the tools that are shared so freely with all who seek freedom there.

Detachment means so many things. It will be helpful to list a few more of the principles I will discuss before going any further:

- It's freedom from relying on others to complete our lives.

- It's giving up the victim role.

- It's disengagement from the chaos around us.

- It may simply be remaining quiet.

- It's not needing attention from others to feel okay.

- It's never letting someone else control how we feel, think, or behave.

- It's giving up the role of being someone else's higher power.

- It's the freedom to not be angry or sad.

I could go on, but the underlying point is always the same: detachment is freedom. And it leads to peace of mind. Always.

My life will simply never be the same since meeting Sheri, Nettie, Marilee, and Janet. Each of us grew up in the midst of family dysfunction, and we lived tumultuous lives for many years because we allowed loved ones to "take over our lives." But finally we all sought the guidance of others who also understood the trauma of lives that were interrupted by the disease of alcoholism, mental illness, violence, and myriad other forms of abuse. And for that I am grateful. The search we all made for help gave me the opportunity to learn from them what I so desperately needed to know.

I have mentioned each of them when discussing some of the other "gifts" we receive as the result of surviving our dysfunctional families; I want to focus specifically on this one gift now because it is so rich in what it offers, as will be detailed through their stories with more of my own woven in. Sometimes it's easiest to define a term by its opposite. This may be true for detachment if, up until now, it's been an unfamiliar term to you. I found its meaning easiest to grasp when I thought about "attachment" and how easily I always got attached to the behaviors of others. I had been able to see, since childhood, that how others behaved affected how I felt.

Seeing its opposite: attachment, as the culprit, can help to define it.

This was true in my family and in every significant relationship. Unfortunately, it had also been true with many of the unsavory alliances I had formed. If you were part of my drama, in any way, you had rent-free space in my mind, as we say in twelve-step rooms. That is nothing to point to with pride. But it's a state that was familiar, I was soon to discover, among the many women I was meeting on my new path, a path that was leading me to a very new understanding about how to live more peacefully.

I have shared much in earlier chapters about each of the women I'm mentioning here, but I have to highlight the finesse they demonstrated with the detachment principle for your benefit and mine. I have learned that every time I recall the strengths that others possess, I am helped to gain strength too. I turn to Sheri first because her family of origin was replete with dysfunction across generations. Her grandparents, their parents too, and of course her own parents, were all affected by alcoholism and drug addiction. Everyone was constantly reacting to one another, she said, and she came into the recovery rooms feeling utter hopelessness.

When a counselor suggested Al-Anon, she was furious, she said. "They are the sick ones! Why should I get help?" And when she came to her first meeting she was even more convinced, she said, that there was no help there for her. Much like my initial reaction, walking into a room where hugging and laughter are present just doesn't add up. These folks *can't* understand my problem! But Sheri stayed, which was a gift to me when I arrived, and for so many others. She was a quick study. The years of abuse, physical and sexual, that she had lived through didn't make her completely jaded. She truly wanted a different experience of life, and she stuck around and got it.

Detachment is giving up the victim role.

Since I arrived after her, I got to skate on her coattails. I have no doubt that knowing Sheri, and the other women too, quickened my recovery. Hearing Sheri talk about the family disease and the way to live unaffected by it gave me hope. She didn't pretend it was easy. She did say one had to be vigilant. I understood vigilance. I had vigilantly watched others to see how I should feel and behave for years. This was simply putting my vigilance to another use. One of Sheri's main suggestions was to walk away from the chaos. Her experience had taught her there would always be chaos. She also stressed that one shouldn't stomp away, even though that might feel desirable. Just quietly walking away would empower us, she said. And it did. I could feel it the very first time I tried it.

Sheri was strong, determined, and soft, all at the same time. She understood the sadness so many in the rooms felt and had risen above the hopelessness that all newcomers feel when they first arrive. She knew that not giving up was the primary step, coupled with letting go of her preconceived ideas of how others would change. And *when* they would change. In her case, as in many of the cases represented in the twelve-step rooms, those others didn't change at all. But *she* changed. *I* changed. So did Nettie, Marilee, and Janet.

Detachment becomes possible for any one of us if we want it badly enough and if we practice it like our lives depend on it.

Remember, detachment is a loving response to all concerned.

Nettie explained it this way: "I no longer tried to get my husband to change his habits. I loved him as he was, with no more suggestions of what he should do. I went to three or four meetings a week and left him alone. And even though he never stopped drinking, our household quieted down and I could laugh again." She also said she was certain he appreciated the change in her because he became far more loving and respectful. Just not more sober. Surprisingly, it didn't matter anymore, she said. Being at peace herself was satisfying enough. And where did her peace come from? She said it came from backing away from all that she had tried to control. She learned very quickly, she said, that God was driving her bus, not her. And that give her a new lease on life, and a peaceful heart.

This is one of the great miracles of what happens when we change our perception and our behavior: what had mattered so much really doesn't anymore. We aren't in denial; we are simply more accepting of those situations and those people we can't control. Letting go, detaching from the behavior of others, changes everything once we get the hang of it.

Allowing others to define their own journey is the kindest gift we can give them.

Listening to Marilee talk about her family of origin and how she changed in regard to them was inspiring, to say the least. The alcoholism was multigenerational, as is generally true, but having siblings who were extremely ill too, and in total denial, made her very sad. For years she suffered alone, not knowing what to do, and then one night saw a public service announcement on television that mentioned Al-Anon if someone in your family was "a problem drinker." Telling no one, she looked in the yellow pages and found her first meeting. She intentionally went to a neighboring town, she said, for fear she'd see someone she knew. And she did, even there. She laughs when she tells the story now, and says she and that woman decided to sponsor each other. Both had sought to "hide" the family problem from others, and found each other.

Understanding the finer points of detachment proved to be very hard for Marilee. She so easily got her feelings hurt by others' behavior that being able to ignore it took time and a herculean effort. She was a southern girl from Alabama, where women had "their place." This was new territory for her. It was a level of assertiveness that she had never attempted. Having a friend in the group and discussing how they could support each other in making changes in their behavior was the key to real growth, Marilee said. It still took time and lots of practice. But everyone I spoke to, and my own experiences too, suggest that nothing changes if nothing changes. Old behavior will not result in new experiences.

For Marilee, the first new detachment behavior she practiced was to not react, in fact, to not interact at all, with family members when they had been drinking. She said she found ways to "be away" when the drinking began, even if it was only to go to her bedroom because she needed a nap. She said it was terribly hard at first, because doing this felt unfamiliar. Being in the midst of the chaos, even when she couldn't control it, was where she had always been. Staying away made her feel left out at first. But after a time she felt a new freedom. She could rejoin the group when she felt ready and could even interact, but didn't have to. That was the miracle. She didn't have to!

....

It's disengagement from the chaos around us.

....

It is our choice whether or not to be in the thick of the confusion of drinking. We don't realize we have made that choice, usually, because we have done it so naturally. But hearing others in "the rooms" talk about the kinds of choices they make gives us newcomers courage to reexamine our habitual choices. And I have discovered that even though I am no longer a newcomer, haven't been for decades, in fact, I need reminders, even today, that I can avoid interaction if it appears to be leading to a place I'd rather not go. This constant process is one of the real gifts of these rooms. We never graduate; we never reach a stage where we can't still learn. And those who are coming after us need our wisdom just as all of us needed the wisdom of those who were there before us.

Sheri, Nettie, Marilee, and I all supported each other and learned a lot from each other over the years. And I think we all contributed to Janet's growth. She came into the rooms with a great need for help. Like everyone I've talked about in this book, she had grown up in a very dysfunctional family. Her experiences were deeply complicated by sexual abuse as a child—abuse that her parents refused to believe or even acknowledge. She was left to wonder if she had imagined it. When she got a bit older she dared to query her brother, and he admitted it. Still, her parents wanted to hear nothing about it.

The fact that she developed her own addictions wasn't surprising. Research indicates that 80 to 85 percent of all women who are sexually abused become addicts. Janet reflected the norm. But after her own solid recovery, her life was troubled by a son who was an addict, a mentally ill husband, and family members who simply relied on her too much for their well-being. She got too easily talked into doing for others what they needed to do for themselves. Detachment as a way of life was truly a life-saving practice for her. But she didn't adjust to it very quickly or easily. Being reminded to "let go" saved her sanity, she says today. It sounds so easy, but the practice of it is anything but easy at the start.

Detachment is giving up the role of being someone else's Higher Power.

I don't think anyone embraces detachment without a lot of prodding. It seems so much more natural for us to "mind other people's business." Offering opinions and solutions, whether they are sought or not, is a knee-jerk reaction for many of us. Even after decades in Al-Anon I have to remember that there is my business and everyone else's business. Unless asked for an opinion, my proper response is *none*. Only then can I truly experience peace of mind.

Every experience we have, every day of our lives, is giving us an opportunity to detach from business that is not ours to mind.

Honoring Detachment as a Life-Giving Force   **111**

The joy of learning to live detached from the problems others have is unfathomable until we have experienced it. It seems unnatural and uncaring, particularly to those of us who are caregivers. And yet letting others have their own journey is the most loving thing we can do. It's the only way we will ever experience joy ourselves. The problems others have are the very learning experiences they need to move forward. When we try to steer the journey of our loved ones, we shortchange them. We miss out on something we need to learn too. We can't be involved in two lives at once. That's God's role. Never ours.

I realize how graced my life is after spending hours with Sheri, Marilee, Nettie and Janet, talking about the good that came from our families of origin and the blessing that is guaranteed by practicing the principle of detachment. Every experience we have or will ever have offers a lesson—learn it now or later. Learning how to practice detachment is the most helpful lesson I have ever experienced. Its application is unlimited. No one need ever upset us again. How freeing is that? How hope-filled is that? How quietly promising is that? Life will never look the same once a person gets the real hang of detachment.

This particular chapter will for certain change your life and all your relationships. That's a guarantee I can make. All you have to do is be willing to allow the suggestions that follow offer you guidance and support:

- Remember, detachment is a loving response to all concerned.

- Allowing others to define their own journey is the kindest gift we can give them.

- Seeing its opposite, *attachment,* as the culprit can help to define it.

- We can experience no peace of mind unless we let others go to live their own lives.

- Every experience we have, every day of our lives, is giving us an opportunity to detach from business that is not ours to mind.

Only then can we fully live the life that we have been blessed with.

As I said earlier in the body of this chapter, detachment is many things:

It's freedom from relying on others to complete our lives.

It's giving up the victim role for one that is far more fulfilling.

It's disengagement from the chaos around us. Walking away is the simplest remedy.

It may simply be remaining quiet—a very effective choice for most of us.

It's not needing attention from others to feel okay, regardless of how good or bad the day is in other respects.

It's never letting someone else control how we feel, think, or behave, which means knowing how to shrug off the actions of others.

It's giving up the role of being someone else's higher power—letting go at last.

It's the freedom not to be angry or sad, instead choosing the emotion we want to cultivate.

The one word that describes detachment the best is FREEDOM. We are free from the confusion of everyone else's life.

Further Reflection

Have I become practiced at detaching from the lives of others? Is there evidence from my recent past that I successfully let others be who they needed to be to do what they needed to do? If not, can I "replay" an experience in my mind so that I can show up in a loving, but detached, way in future encounters?

Do I regularly enjoy peace of mind? And if I don't, can I see how and where my behavior could change so that I do experience more peace?

10

Listening from the Heart

Friends are those rare people who ask how we are, and then wait to hear the answer.

Ed Cunningham

Listening from the heart is listening with *intention*. It's listening with *complete attention*. Intention and attention, related and yet different, are key to being present to the travelers who have been sent our way. It's our gift to them to be attentive, while their joining our circle has been their gift to us. The give and take is a never ending exchange.

How good a listener are you? Most of us probably consider ourselves relatively good listeners, but are we really? Do we look into the eyes of the person who is speaking? Do we wait to hear the end of what he or she is saying before formulating our own response? How often do we turn our minds away, assuming we know what they are going to say before they have finished the sentence or the idea?

I fight against this tendency all too often. And yet, I think being in the rooms of recovery has been helpful in curbing my tendency to let my mind wander, because in our circles we share ourselves so intimately that to not honor one another with listening is truly disrespectful, one of the traits many of us are working to change.

Not being listened to is a familiar feeling for many of us, unfortunately. Even though we may be long gone from our family of origin, we may have chosen friends and life partners who treat us much like our families did, and it goes without saying that many of us grew up in families that didn't listen to what we had to say. We get accustomed to certain treatment, and as the saying goes, *we inadvertently teach others how to treat us.* If we want to be treated differently, we need to raise our expectations. In some cases, we may even have to make suggestions to those around us.

Clearly, one of the most effective ways of encouraging others to listen to us is by demonstrating our willingness to listen to them. Let's review what listening really entails:

- It's being completely, unabashedly attentive.

- It's being a witness, in the fullest sense of the term, to the person standing before us.

- It's dismissing all unrelated thoughts that wander through our minds while a friend is talking to us.

- If we find ourselves beginning to lose focus, we immediately refocus on the person speaking, remembering that he or she is a visitor *sent by God* in that very moment. This is a most compelling idea, I think.

Our traveling companions are *never* accidentally walking by our side. We made pacts with them to be teachers and students to one another long before we were born. That may strike you as odd, even unfathomable. But I have decided to honor this idea, one I was introduced to by Carolyn Myss, a spiritual intuitive, because of how well it explains, and softens, the experiences I have lived through. What I have learned and then passed on to others has benefitted many, I think. I'm inclined to think that's why we have our many and varied experiences. They are not just for our edification alone.

And even if I don't have a complete understanding of how and why others appeared on my path, and how the learning process works, I have chosen to think it really doesn't matter. We are here. We share the path with others. And we learn specific things that, in time, we tell many others about. They get to learn from our experiences, just as we have learned from the experiences of people who were sent to us. It's a cycle of life and learning, and it gets repeated over and over. This mystical, magical principle satisfies many of my questions.

Listening is one aspect of that cycle, and some would say it should receive priority treatment. It's such a gift we give others when we truly listen to them. And it's such *an honor* to be heard. I doubt that any one of you who might be reading this book grew up in a family that gave you the full loving attention you deserved, that *heard* you in the way you wanted and needed to be heard. Had that been the case, you probably wouldn't have found a book about dysfunctional families appealing.

But most families are dysfunctional in some way. And most family members, in general, pay very little serious attention to one another, seldom taking particular notice of one another's presence, let alone asking each other intimate, thoughtful questions and then waiting for answers.

Am I being too hard on the ordinary family? I think not, unfortunately.

....

Listening is a gift that requires a simple decision.

....

I find it really disturbing that we can live in such close proximity to one another and yet so far from one another's heart and soul. But I have also come to believe that that's one of the primary lessons we are here to experience. Our lives aren't about *seeing the material body* of one another, but rather experiencing each other's *inner* presence. And we do that with our hearts. Of all the people I spoke to in preparing for the writing of this book, no one felt more invisible and had more of a "heartfelt" story to share than Marilee.

To reiterate, she grew up with alcoholic chaos. Listening was not a trait anyone possessed in her house. Anyone but her, that is. She often felt bereft and frightened. And definitely lonely. Her marriage, though not to an alcoholic, mimicked her family of origin in many ways. She had no listener. He was a workaholic. She grew so accustomed to the distance between them that she doubted she had anything to say that was worth hearing. Had it not been for the extremely dangerous and somewhat depraved alcoholic behavior of a sister, she may never have sought the help that was to change her life.

Marilee was a natural at listening, perhaps to a fault. Had she been less attentive to the many sick souls in her family, she might have escaped some of the pain of her family of origin. Her attention to everyone and their constant and demanding needs shredded her emotional state. She came to "us," desperate and willing to go to any lengths to find solace, deeply needing to be heard.

We were eager to help. The people in recovery rooms are always eager to help, and listening is high on the agenda.

We have learned to listen from the heart and our soft, expressive attentiveness reveals our commitment to being fully present. There is no judgment when one listens from the heart. And freedom from judgment is our goal. Marilee needed validating, more than almost anything else, and having someone attentively listening was a gratifying way of achieving that validation. Because Marilee followed the suggestion to get a sponsor, she began learning the many tools for living the serene life. And in this sponsor she found a loving listener, at last.

Marilee mastered the tools that made her life so much more tolerable, even joyful. As mentioned, she was soon to be a successful practitioner of detachment, a great example to many of us of the fruits of "walking away" when our attention isn't needed. Her example of kindness to others showed us what it should look like. She came into the rooms with much to forgive, and she allowed us to observe her process. By doing so, we were all helped in our own practice of forgiveness. Perhaps the one quality Marilee wore most obviously was her uncommon expression of oneness. She welcomed you into her "world" with her eyes, her open arms, and her smile. You had no doubt, whatsoever, that Marilee was with you all of the way. She was listening to your every word, your every cry for help, and your every expression of joy.

....

Heartfelt listening is always without judgment.

....

To be loved without judgment is such a gift. Seldom can a person who grew up in a dysfunctional home claim they were raised without judgment being heaped on them. And when judgment is the predominant thread that runs through the family, each person in the family fails miserably at listening from the heart. They simply feel too vulnerable, too fragile. Severe judgment and heartfelt listening are quite clearly antithetical. Marilee was judged as too serious—too quick to see a problem where no one else saw one. She was a troublemaker, some said. She retreated, painfully doubting her vision, until she came to Al-Anon, where she found the support, the clarification, and the validation that had so long been missing from her life.

I felt this same lack of loving attention in my family of origin too. I got attention, but it was far more shaming than loving. I was always acting out, so the family's response to me wasn't the kind of attention that served as an invitation to sit and share what was happening in my life or how I felt inside. Never did that happen. Never. I doubt that my parents had ever even considered doing that.

....

Intentional listening is always single-mindedly focused.

....

Making the decision to listen requires steadfastness and clear-headedness. It sounds so easy, but most of us have gotten so lazy in our efforts to stay focused. We have also gotten very self-centered, being rooted in *our personal search for love and acceptance.* That's the natural response for the "dysfunction" we suffered from. We watch others to see if they "see us," rather than unselfishly turning our attention to them. Wanting to be the center of someone else's life made sense to us.

How grateful everyone I spoke with has become since learning that there is another way to experience life.

Developing an appreciation for others, honoring the inner knowledge that whoever is present has come intentionally—this can change every moment of one's life. I no longer doubt that every minute is sacred, and this awareness has changed my perspective completely.

This discussion now brings to mind an individual I have yet to introduce, a woman I grew to admire tremendously. Her name is Patty and she came into the recovery rooms desperate, having an adult son and a twin sister who were addicts. Like everyone else in this book, she didn't have good role models as parents. She wasn't seriously listened to as a youngster and she made many mistakes. A major one was her first husband. After marrying him, she was consumed with the actions of other people for decades, and that, coupled with her own serious health problems, made her very vulnerable to the whims of others. A counselor sent her to Al-Anon, a suggestion she initially resented. Like so many of us, she figured the others in her life were the sick ones. Why did she need to commit to a program? However, out of desperation, she went.

I happened to be at Patty's first meeting. She had the look of exhaustion coupled with desperation in her eyes. She resembled so many of us when we first seek help. Her eyes darted around the room, looking for a familiar face, no doubt. We don't really want to see someone we know, and yet we fear the unfamiliarity. I would have guessed she heard very little at that first meeting, but we heard her plea without her even giving voice to the words racing through her mind. We had all been there. Many of us were still there, some days.

Following the meeting, she approached me and asked if I could explain some of the terminology. That began a friendship that has survived for many years. Much has happened in Patty's family since her arrival to our "rooms." The sister took her own life and the son has yet to maintain his sobriety, but Patty stands as an example to all of us of what change looks like, what developing a relationship with a Higher Power looks like, and what peace, one day at a time, looks like too.

Listening is an art that needs continuous practice. Continuous.

When I asked Patty what contributed most to the obviously changed woman we all observed, she said it was being willing to listen to those she now walked among. She said she had tried many things, none of which worked, before "sitting in these rooms." And now, little by little, her mind and heart had changed. Being humble enough to listen to the suggestions others made, and then being willing to truly allow others to see who she was, at her worst and her best, gave her the courage to continue following the lead of others who were living lives far more contented than her own.

Listening is no small feat, as has already been established. Extraneous thoughts can interfere continuously. I've learned that this is the ego trying to pull me away from God's messages. I have become convinced that the ego never sleeps. In order to make the next right decision or take the next kind action, I must be vigilant about my willingness to listen to the subtle and kind voice of God, as it is often heard through the other people on my path.

Patty proved to be a role model in due time. She showed through her actions and words that she had retained the wisdom of the many men and women in the recovery circles she so readily clung to. That's the turning point for any one of us, isn't it? If we listen intently to the wise, we will grow. Our behavior will change. Our hearts and minds will be renewed. I am a living example of this. I must say it again: nothing changes if nothing changes, and one of the easiest changes we can make is being willing to listen intently to those who are crossing our path. *They are there by design.* Even those individuals who trouble us—from them we generally learn the most!

Patty has gone on to nurture so many others and is a natural as "a teacher" of this new way of seeing and living. One of the women she has had an impact on happens to be another person I interviewed for this book. I'll call her Marilyn. She is a survivor. That was the first obvious realization I had when she began to share her story with me. It was fortunate that I had made a commitment to listening as part of my program, too, because the tale she shared was almost unbelievable. However, I knew every word was true. Every single horrific word.

Marilyn's father was a psychiatrist. Her mother was well educated too, as were her many siblings. But what went on inside the home was unfathomable. Her father had monstrous outbursts. They often culminated in beatings of her mother, followed by complete denial that what they had observed had ever happened. Because of her father's power in the community and at the university where he practiced, it seemed impossible for the family to protect themselves in any public way, or confront the situation as it should have been confronted. Everyone just moved on after each incident, trying to put it behind them, trying to soothe their hurt, their bruises, their confused psyches.

Marilyn didn't succeed in letting it go, however. Her response as she grew up was to act out. And her acting out became what the family focused on, rather than the very ill father. It's not unusual for this kind of situation to occur in a highly dysfunctional family. Someone becomes the scapegoat, and Marilyn almost eagerly grabbed at that role and fulfilled it to a tee. It didn't help the family's dysfunction but it did give her mother something else to focus on.

Seeking help and being listened to are the first steps on the road to healing.

By the time Marilyn came for help she had been through a number of programs for her addictions. The remaining problem was her attachment to extremely unhealthy men, which was not surprising considering what she had grown up expecting from the opposite sex. I became interested in her story for this book, not because she had made much progress yet in the recovery rooms, but because she was a great example of the "before" in a before and after comparison. When she entered recovery, all you had to do was ask her a couple of questions and you'd note very quickly that every answer seemed rehearsed. Someone else's life seemed to be at the center of every response she made. She was a woman who lived on the fringes of her own life and clearly tried to live at the center of everyone else's life.

I had known this syndrome first hand, unfortunately. And yet, I recovered. I knew she could recover too. I made the decision to begin talking with Marilyn often so I could observe her behavior in all the stages of change that I was sure she'd experience. I questioned; I watched; I listened. For weeks and months. And the forward movement was very slow. I realized that some have a much harder time changing than others. The inner turmoil is more ingrained, perhaps; the fear over who we might become if we choose new patterns of responding to the world around us simply keeps us stuck. Marilyn seemed stuck. And for a time, she stopped visiting the recovery rooms.

When she returned, she showed marked improvement. She had sought help from a gifted therapist and no longer seemed caught in the web of her family. She also learned healthier habits through her friendship with Patty, which makes such a difference in her life. They both had very ill family members, and Patty had learned how to observe and detach. Marilyn was learning this too.

How is detachment related to listening? Detachment is the hallmark of any healthy relationship. Being able to detach appropriately is the hallmark of an individual's mental and spiritual health. But it's important here to establish that detachment doesn't imply we quit listening to or paying attention to one another. Detachment simply means we aren't defined by the actions or opinions of others. It's an important distinction.

I want to return to Sheri's experiences for a time because she was a stellar example of a person who listened intently to the stories of others but was able to maintain a healthy detachment at the same time. That's partially because she listened without judgment and without the inclination to direct. She listened with a heart that was always open, which enabled her to love those around her while they were cultivating a better mental and spiritual condition. And she was a help to others in spite of the severely grave circumstances she lived in. Her ability to detach from the grasp of her own unhealthy family made it possible for her to be available to the needs of others.

We learn so much from one another. I first visited the recovery rooms quite ignorant of the principles I have discussed in this book. When I joined Al-Anon in 1974, all I had in my favor was the willingness to seek a different way to experience my relationships and life circumstances. I sought that different way because the pain in my life was palpable. But that's all it takes: willingness. For most of us, the pain needs to be excessive, like mine was, or we wouldn't be willing to change.

There are many skills we can learn from one another. Listening may be one of the hardest.

Listening seems simple, but it's elusive. I think the practice of deep listening is comparable to meditation. We have to bring our minds back to center again and again, without judging ourselves for wandering. Practice makes listening more manageable and tangible. The more intently we listen, the more knowledge we acquire. We become more enlightened. The payoff is as palpable as the pain had been.

Not to be heard, to be actively dismissed, can be devastating. I want to include some of Janet's story in this chapter because this injustice was done to her as a young girl when no one listened to her story of abuse. Her parents and sisters didn't want to know about it. But what had happened was not imaginary. Her brother had forced himself on her when she was too young to know what it actually meant. She only knew it must be wrong because he made her promise not to tell or he'd do it over and over. She never told until she was in her late teens, and then her revelation was met with deaf ears and no response. *None at all.*

Getting no response seemed so unfathomable that she had to wonder, had they really not heard her anguish? She wondered if she had simply imagined she'd told them. With the help of a therapist, she finally gathered the courage, *and it took a great deal of it*, to approach her brother. He listened. He didn't deny the abuse. Janet was so relieved that she found it far easier to forgive him than she had imagined it would be. He was truly sorry and asked to be forgiven. Janet's parents still refused to acknowledge the truth, even as it was once again presented to them. It haunted Janet that she was not heard regarding such a serious matter. That fact of her childhood informed so much of her life. She chose life partners who were equally as dismissive. It wasn't until she found the rooms of Al-Anon for help regarding a child of her own that she found real understanding and healing over the circumstances of her own childhood.

There is simply no way to overestimate the healing power of listening.

Whether we recall Patty's story, Marilee's, William's, or Janet's, the absence of a parent or older sibling who lovingly listens can open the door to a life of unnecessary trauma and strife. We all have a great need to be heard. And when this need goes unmet, we may seek attention in unhealthy ways. At the very least, we have an emptiness inside that will seek to be filled in some way. You have already heard how I tried to fill my emptiness. All the men and women I have told you about in these pages tried to fill their "holes" similarly, through attachments to drugs, alcohol, sex, gambling, people, or all the above. Not until we finally give up in desperation do we seek the only help that really heals. And the solution has been there waiting for us all along.

What is this one solution for the emptiness that haunts millions? It is found in the circles each of these folks eventually discovered. A room full of listeners is the balm that finally heals. It's so simple and yet so elusive until we begin to trust it. Listening, as already established, sounds so simple, but it takes willingness, again and again. We didn't learn how to do it at the knees of our parents but we are in the process of being "re-parented" by the wise men and women on our path. Now we too can "re-parent" others by giving them our loving, constant, and undivided attention. Today is a new day. Today will usher to us those who need a listener. Let's be there.

Listening is one readily accessible solution that will lessen the pain of the person who wanders across our path.

Listening is a gift that requires a simple decision.

Intentional listening is always single-mindedly focused.

Heartfelt listening is without judgment.

Some think listening is an art than needs continuous practice. I, for one, agree.

Seeking help and being heard is the first step on the road to healing.

There are many skills we learn from one another. Listening may be one of the hardest to master.

Further Reflection

Listening can be considered a safety net for all of us—a safety net that's needed in a profound way. Had we been listened to as youngsters, we'd have chosen partners who were healthier, no doubt. But it's never too late to begin a new way to live. Listening to each sacred soul who wanders our way is the solution; both theirs and ours. And it's not rocket science. It relies on the cultivation of a quiet mind and a willing heart. Both are attainable. Now.

11

Seeing the Trap in Judgment and the Release in Acceptance

Can you look without the voice in your head commenting, drawing conclusions, comparing, or trying to figure something out?

Eckhart Tolle

Passing judgment on another person's perspective, opinion, suggestion, appearance, or behavior is an act of separation. Some might consider it an attack that results in the disharmony that is at the core of human frailty and the ultimate unease of our communities. That the community, like the individual, is affected makes sense, but the disharmony can't be contained to the few. It eventually spreads throughout the country too, like a dreaded epidemic. We can sense this lack of harmony every time we turn on cable television or talk radio. The voices are often shrill, argumentative, or downright belligerent. And the retorts often match them in volume and vitriol.

If we want to experience peace in our lives, and this is the choice I have made, we have to be vigilant against adding to the disharmony all around us. We do this through adopting a number of simple practices. The first one, and perhaps the easiest one that comes to mind, is "stepping aside" rather than letting our minds, coupled with our actions, become engaged with others in a negative way. Getting caught up in someone's negative behavior, inadvertently absorbing his or her negative opinions, is a choice. It may be a passive choice, but it's a choice nonetheless. However, we can choose *to look the other way*, or at the very least, move our minds away from the "chaos" and say nothing. When seriously practiced, this is not a difficult choice.

....

The choice for peace, rather than judgment, is worth the effort we give it.

....

Unbridled negativity of any kind can give birth to unnecessary and unkind judgment of our fellow travelers. We forget, in the moment that the conflict has arisen, that we are "companions by choice," not by accident. We share the stage to learn from one another, not to sit in judgment of one another. It's good that our companions have, and freely share, opinions that we don't embrace ourselves. We are stretched by our willingness to be tolerant of the viewpoints of others. I have come to treasure the fact that people unlike me have been great teachers of tolerance, patience, acceptance, and finally, love. Who would have ever guessed that love could be one of the gifts owing to our differences?

Being with our teachers every moment of every day provides the opportunities we need to practice acceptance rather than judgment, a crucial practice if we want to be comforted by the interactions we experience, rather than set on edge. Acceptance of others, all situations, and every experience helps to heal our individual wounds, which in turn heals the wounds of humankind. Acceptance, practiced at a profoundly deep level, is the solution to the angry discourse that has infected the human community.

Our teachers are everywhere. When we allow them to be present, free of our judgment, this propels us to a new understanding of acceptance first, then peace.

Dysfunctional families live in a maelstrom of judgment, which infects every situation facing each family member throughout the day. Carl's home life was a perfect example of this intense turmoil because of the extremely negative dominance of Carl's dad. His dominance weighed heavily on family members, but no one was affected as gravely as Carl, whose spirit was nearly extinguished in childhood. Had it not been for a loving wife who masterfully reignited his dying spirit in the early years of their marriage, Carl might have succumbed to an early death.

It's far too easy to dismiss the impact judgment can have on a person's psyche—his interior spaces. When the judgment is constant, as was the case in Carl's home, emotional exhaustion sets in, and the drive to succeed at anything is diminished. As mentioned in an earlier chapter, Carl had no drive to excel in school or on the job when first employed. However, being fired was the catalyst that opened new doors and propelled Carl to succeed in a new town, at a new job, giving him the freedom to be who he really was: a soft, gentle soul who didn't want to live in a state of conflict with anyone. His wife's demonstration of acceptance was his model for change.

And what did she do exactly? Carl said she showered him with loving gestures every day; she encouraged him to "stretch" on the job; she complimented his achievements, even small ones; and she made sure he knew how very much she loved him *as he was.* In no small measure, Amy helped to heal the very deep wounds that had been tearing at him since childhood. Carl couldn't fully express his debt of gratitude to her, but he tried. You couldn't possibly miss the signs of affection that passed between them.

Dysfunctional families practice so many unfavorable behaviors, scathing judgment being only one of many, that it's nearly unfathomable that folks can rise, as they do, to become people of great charm and achievement, committed to persevering towards specific goals, and determined to develop and reveal qualities that were foreign to them in their family of origin. One wonders how this is even possible. After years of reflection, I've come to believe that actually, everything is possible because of the presence of a God of our understanding who simply awaits our call for help. And having learned that the solution to any problem is being willing to accept every moment as perfect and orchestrated by God for the growth relieves us of any fear that might linger in the recesses of our minds. Acceptance simply changes every mountain into a tiny hill—one that we can climb with grace and strength and joy.

I observed acute powers of acceptance in every interviewee for this book. And I knew within moments of beginning the interviews that each person had lived in an environment bereft of acceptance. When fear is the basis of family dynamics, acceptance can't find fertile ground for development. Acceptance must take root in the right circumstances, from a base of love rather than fear.

Acceptance is the quiet solution to every unwelcome circumstance or person that can't be changed or controlled—in a family, a community, a country.

In a family environment that is severely judgmental, one of the many good qualities that we can develop is an eagerness for acceptance. It's fascinating to me that the lack of acceptance I lived with in my family of origin propelled me to demonstrate my acceptance of folks who were quite unlike the family in which I was reared. Was there a connection? I think yes. The more judgment I felt, the more I wanted to establish that I was making different choices, and this is not unusual. In fact, many of my interviewees expressed the same willingness to be extremely accepting of others.

Marilee comes to mind again. She amazed me with her profound expression of quiet acceptance. It was not only her family of origin that she found difficult to survive, but her marriage too. She went from the frying pan into the fire, as the saying goes. And yet she held her head high and never lost the grace with which she had been blessed. She allowed others to be who they were called to be, and acceptance became second nature to her. It was either that or be miserable all the time.

Because Marilee's family was steeped in alcoholism, and other "isms" too, it chose to be insulated from the outer world. Not wanting others to see inside the family is not uncommon when the system is as diseased as hers was. A dysfunctional family seems to know, at some level, that something is wrong in how they function; they know enough to want to hide it, but simply don't know how to change it. Nor do they really desire to change it. And yet, there is often that one family member who says, "I want something different. I want out." This breaks the system. The one who steps outside of it often becomes a pariah, however. This was the case for Marilee, who chose to marry someone whose behavior and opinions were consistent with her birth family. It is frightening to choose to plant yourself too far from the family tree.

Making a different choice about how to experience the rest of your life is a common theme in a survivor's journey.

Observing her from afar for many months before seeking to interview her, I saw how committed Marilee was to the fullest expression of acceptance. Her acceptance was real and total. Although she had never felt accepted in her family of origin, she developed the willingness to let them be who they were. Her love for them, *as they were,* was sincere. But her involvement with them was selective. She made sure she had an escape plan when a visit was necessary. This was a common thread among the survivors I interviewed. Regardless of how accepting they were, having a ready excuse to leave a setting became mandatory. It's unfortunate to need an escape plan, but knowing what's tolerable and what isn't is a sign of growth.

Every man and woman I interviewed had developed the skill of acceptance to one degree or another. Acceptance was essential to their survival in their families and in the world around them. One has to finally give in to acceptance in order to find even a modicum of peace. Few give in before they have explored all other avenues, however, and that's only reasonable. The one person I spoke with on many occasions who fought giving in harder than most was William.

William, if you will recall, grew up with extremely distant parents to whom he felt no real connection, and a sister who didn't choose to be his confidant either. He felt unattached to all of them, and lost in the family dynamic of unexpressed concern about him or his interests. Fortunately, their lack of interest in him didn't sway him from a commitment to succeeding. During our interview, he wondered out loud if that commitment was designed to get a response from one or both parents. It didn't—they remained aloof and disinterested. Fortunately for William, a teacher or two took notice of his skills, and he got what he craved—attention.

William got that attention in full measure from his first wife, but after her untimely death, wife number two came with her own set of problems. William found it hard to empathize or understand her alcoholism. He had not yet honed the practice of acceptance.

Acceptance doesn't develop naturally for most of us. It grows out of years of frustration, coupled with the kindness of someone who can demonstrate its value to us.

But because he and his second wife had given birth to two children, William found it necessary to make some adjustments to their home life. A man who never looked for help from others (because it was a sign of weakness) was suddenly at a loss. In seeking help, he felt he would be succumbing to a level of weakness that would never have been tolerated in his family of origin. Nonetheless, his love for his children convinced him it was worth it. He wasn't quick to accept the situation at home, and he wasn't keen on it. But he was determined, applying the same determination to excel that he had in sports and schoolwork in his youth.

Determination comes in handy when we are faced with new challenges. I observed this in all of the interviewees for this book. No one was going to suffer defeat. Everyone was absolutely certain that determined perseverance was the key to survival. Being determined to accept others "where they live" is the key to a peaceful journey.

....

Accepting others, regardless of their opinions, their behaviors, and their prejudices moves all the members of the human community to a higher plane of existence.

....

Being "taught" through the guidance of our sponsors and the wise voices in our twelve-step meetings to accept others where they are is one of the finest gifts any one of us can receive. It's likewise quite possibly one of the finest gifts we can model for others. Each time we model it, it roots itself more securely in our psyche.

Choosing acceptance over judgment requires a shift in perception that every peace-filled person has made at some time in his or her life. Memories of my interviews with Nettie jump to my mind. As you will recall, her husband never quit drinking, but she went from being a woman who laughingly said she contemplated homicide to one who expressed the giddiness of constant joy. Even after forty years in Al-Anon, nothing at home changed. But *everything* in her psyche did. That everything boiled down to one concept: acceptance. She opened her mind to the idea of letting her husband be who he was called to be. And she went on living her life, too.

Acceptance of your fellow travelers has the power to change the journey for everyone you meet today. Its power isn't restricted to just the interchange between two individuals. It permeates the encounters both of these individuals have with everyone else too, and travels through additional encounters as well. Every good exchange is paid forward. No one, absolutely no one, is left untouched when it comes to the effect of a change such as this.

Because acceptance is such a powerful antidote to every anxious moment and every potential conflict, I can't express strongly enough what the practice of acceptance would do for the unrest that circles the globe. Perhaps it seems naive to believe that what I say or do here in Minnesota affects someone in Bangladesh, but that's what I believe. And I'm in good company. Some of the wisest spiritual thinkers share my views. Look to the writings of Deepak Chopra, for instance, or the words of the Dalai Lama. Turn to the popular writings of Wayne Dyer and Marianne Williamson. Even Oprah Winfrey believes that what we do to one travels on to many. Therefore, fully accepting one person, totally allowing one person's faults and foibles, grants acceptance to many others too. What an accessible gift for us and our traveling companions.

Acceptance is the gift that keeps on giving.

Finally, let me return to Allison's story. If you recall, Allison was the first to get sober in her large, Irish Catholic alcoholic family. She paved the way for many to follow, including her father. She also paved the way by providing a powerful demonstration of acceptance. Allison embodied acceptance not only of the reactions of the others in her family when she chose to blow the whistle on them, but also of her dire diagnosis of pelvic cancer—a prognosis that left her disabled for life, a few years into her recovery.

My interview with Allison stunned me. As she sat, gently composed in her wheelchair, she talked about what it had been like to grow in acceptance of the many changes she had undergone. Not only has she lost her capacity to walk, but she has also lost her capacity to move freely, even inside her own home. Having young boys at home when this life-altering condition surfaced meant she couldn't be the soccer mom, the room mother, the scout leader. She was different from all the other moms, and her boys resented it at times. Her response was simply to show up in every setting with as much gusto as possible. Acceptance—theirs and hers—didn't come easy. But it came.

And now she represents to hundreds of others who see her in recovery rooms every week, at family functions, and elsewhere, that we are never down without our consent. If ever there was anyone who had a reason for justified resentment, coupled with negative judgment over life's unfair turn of events, it's Allison. But that's not who she is. She shines with a great attitude and a matching sense of humor. Acceptance is the key. She's quick to sing the praises of acceptance, too.

Nothing can hold us back; nothing can hinder our progress for long, if we commit ourselves to developing an attitude of acceptance.

After nearly four decades on the recovery path, I am more firm in my belief now than ever before that nothing happens in our lives by accident. And this belief has made it possible for me, and for the many resilient people I interviewed, to look at our lives as whole, perfect in every way, and sustainable. This belief paves the way to complete acceptance. Had we not been born into heavily dysfunctional families, perhaps our resilience would not be as strong. There is a prize in every box of cracker jacks, if you look for it. There is success within every endeavor if you allow for it. There are miracles around every corner, if you look for them with an open heart and an expectant mind. The offspring of dysfunctional families know these truths to be self-evident.

Before moving ahead with the next growth opportunity owing to our upbringing in a dysfunctional family, let's review all the good stuff that was offered in this chapter. Any one of these keys is life-altering.

> The choice for peace, rather than judgment, is worth the effort we give it.

> Our teachers are everywhere. When we allow them to be present, free of our judgment, this propels us to a new understanding of acceptance first, then peace.

> Acceptance is the quiet solution to every circumstance or person that can't be changed or controlled—in a family, a community, a country.

> Making a different choice about how to experience the rest of your life is a common theme in a survivor's journey.

> Acceptance doesn't develop naturally for most of us. It grows out of years of frustration, coupled with the kindness of someone who can demonstrate its value to us.

Acceptance is the gift that keeps on giving.

Nothing can hold us back. Nothing can hinder our progress for long if we commit ourselves to developing an attitude of acceptance.

Further Reflection

Judgment and acceptance are opposing forces. Whichever one we cultivate will decide the kind of day we will experience; the kind of future we can expect; the kind of relationships we will enjoy; the kind of legacy we will leave behind. Our life is the sum total of every idea we treasure and every action we take. We decide who we are, how we will be recalled, what will be said about us, and what, finally, will be remembered about us. Let's make sure we'll find pleasure in what we leave behind.

12

Being Responsible and Letting Others Be Responsible

Eventually we all have to accept full and total responsibility for our actions, everything we have done, and have not done.

Hubert Selby, Jr.

Taking full responsibility for ourselves is an awesome decision, as well as a humble one. It means growing up in the best sense of the phrase. It means no longer laying the blame on someone else for anything that happens in our lives. It means relishing the moments of peace that come with accepting who we were, and knowing that who we are becoming is still in the developmental stage. The good news about this is as long as we remain in a "state of becoming," we can attain a level of growth. We want to comfortably embrace who we are at every stage; because we continue to grow, we get to embrace ourselves again and again.

We must acknowledge, and this is terribly important, that we hold total responsibility for our failure to take action that might have been beneficial to ourselves or others in days gone by. Even though we ducked the responsibility on many occasions, whatever we were faced with was ours to handle.

It is profoundly empowering to accept responsibility for ourselves, as we are taught to do in our recovery rooms, down to the tiniest of life's details. It feels really good; it sustains us; it prepares us to be even more responsible. We build character each time we choose not to shirk our duty, not to step behind someone else in line when volunteers are needed for the work that benefits humankind. Every time we say yes to a request for help, we are learning the value of taking responsibility.

Offering to be helpful at the right moments, while not stepping in where others need to be in charge, is just one of the many responsible actions we can take.

In days long gone, seldom did we say yes in an effort to truly be helpful. If we said yes, it was quite often manipulative, born out of a desire for control, and thus corrosive. That's the kind of training many of us had in our family of origin. We learned our lessons well, but fortunately we no longer live in the past. We arise each day with the knowledge that we can make the day a good one for ourselves, and quite possibly others. Taking responsibility for that which is ours is the launching pad we need to fully embrace the person we are crying out to be.

We need not worry about being overly responsible—not this early in the game. Just becoming willing to pick up the load that wears our name is all that's expected. Fortunately, just being alive means we will be faced with these opportunities multiple times a day. Being born into families that are ravaged by dysfunction sends many confusing signals about responsibility, what it entails, how to accept it, and how to give it to others when it is clearly not ours to take.

I certainly grew up in the midst of confusion about who was to blame for the disharmony in our home. My mother's sullenness, often to the point of bitterness, was her attempt to punish my dad, I think, for his constant tone of belittlement or outright rage. Both she and my younger brother were generally on the receiving end of the rage. And Dad certainly never took responsibility for his anger. It was always because one of us had failed to do something, or anything at all, right. Trying to stay under the radar of his rage simply wasn't possible. He shot from the hip, and one of us was always the target.

Observing the many times others fail to take responsibility, when they are clearly responsible, offers us many helpful lessons.

Many of those I interviewed had learned when and how to accept responsibility. Those who were still prone to moving in too readily to take charge were working on standing back, taking a thoughtful pause before acting, and allowing others to pick up the task if it was theirs to pick up. Being overly responsible becomes easy, I think, because it makes us look busy and feel good—worthy of the affection of others. This is an insidious self-assessment bestowed on us in our very misguided families.

It was a pleasure to observe and talk with many who were changing this family dynamic for themselves, and in the families they were raising. Recovery fosters an incredible ability to break the mold. Nearly every one of us has inhabited moments of being overly responsible on the one hand or shirking our responsibility on the other, and we can break out of both extremes.

I got great joy from talking with William about responsibility. As you recall, he was raised in a cold, detached Scandinavian family where he observed very unemotional over-responsibility as an ordinary, everyday trait. That, of course, taught him to model the same behavior. However, when he matured, his overly responsible behavior became overly controlling, which he carried into his first marriage and unfortunately, into the second one. Being overly controlling is never well received, not even by those individuals who shirk their own responsibility at every opportunity.

It's not always easy to tell the difference between being controlling and taking a bit too much responsibility.

We have to be willing to check our motives, constantly, to assess what our actions really mean. Are we stepping up to the plate to look good, to make sure things go our way, or because it's really our turn to step up? In William's case, he stepped up because he wanted everything to line up with his expectations, and when one's marriage partner is a practicing alcoholic, you can kiss your expectations goodbye.

William despaired at how day after day unfolded, and this brought him into Al-Anon. The best thing about his demeanor when he came was that he was exhausted, truly spent. He had tried everything he could think of, and had been defeated again and again. Even though it was the last thing he wanted to do, he had effectively recreated his family of origin. All warmth toward his wife had left him. Fortunately he still loved his boys very much, but he simply wanted his wife to get with the program. His cold judgment mirrored that of his only family of origin. He tried controlling the situation, insisting his wife be more responsible, but this didn't produce the results he wanted.

We can never force responsibility onto another person. We can only be willing to volunteer ourselves.

William was a steady student, however. Attending seven to ten meetings a week made him capable of practicing the suggestions the program offered very quickly. He absorbed the idea, perhaps by osmosis through near constant exposure, that being overly responsible as a parent and husband wasn't going to change the circumstances of his wife's drinking. She would have to be responsible for that choice herself. He had to let go of everything he had learned in his family of origin about being responsible, what it meant, and how far one had to take it. Only then could real growth, lasting growth, be triggered in his family. Little by little, day after day, he practiced his new behaviors: "stepping aside," rather than constantly suggesting what others should do; letting go of outcomes rather than pouting over how things developed; giving his wife the freedom to drink or not. In near record time, changes began to happen at home. We can never be certain they will last. That's the hard part—but we can only be certain that our own behavior is held in check. We remain responsible for ourselves. Period.

Patty demonstrated incredible clarity about who was and wasn't responsible for whatever happened. The dysfunction in her family of origin was no greater or less than that in any other family I was introduced to; however, her willingness to change how she saw her family members, and then herself, was attained at record speed. She hated how she felt every day when she awoke. She was tired out by the previous day's attempts to control, to be responsible in areas that were clearly none of her business.

By the time she came to the rooms of recovery, she was exhausted. Not unlike so many of us, her dedication to controlling everything didn't allow for many rest-filled days or nights. And because she had alcoholics all around her, she felt driven to control what was never controllable. Assuming responsibility for the actions or inactions of others was second nature to her. But of course she was never appreciated for all she did for her family.

Doing for others what they must do themselves is never really appreciated. We do what we must do for ourselves.

Patty brought humor to the rooms. She shared great stories about her own failed boundaries and her overzealous attempts to be responsible for the finer details of the many lives she encountered daily. She could laugh at herself for behavior so unbecoming to one who was letting go. But she just couldn't get the hang of letting her sister and her children be responsible for themselves. Without her help she felt they'd not survive, for sure. Sadly, her sister didn't survive. But because Patty had the rooms for support, she continued to grow and help the rest of us grow, even through this deeply painful experience. Through her experiences, she showed us the stark differences between one's own personal responsibility and someone else's responsibility. With her children, her son in particular, she practiced this lesson well.

As she is wont to say, what he does is his business. She never asks. She never offers. She only listens and takes charge of what is hers to be in charge of. Hearing her say she has no idea if he is sober and clean, nor does she care, is a great lesson for everyone to hear. Her response is always, "I love him. Period. Sober and clean or not." Patty has learned what her responsibilities are, and what they are not. And she has no trouble sticking with her own.

What's good about this is that we get to see someone be happy in spite of the behavior of loved ones. We get to see the joy in backing away from taking on someone else's responsibilities. And we get to see the joy Patty expresses in fulfilling what *is* her responsibility, part of which is to love her son regardless of his choices.

....

Accepting responsibility where appropriate, and not taking it on where inappropriate, is evidence of good boundaries, good balance, and emotional maturity.

....

Not every one advances as quickly in this particular arena. Valerie would probably agree that she finds letting others be wholly responsible for themselves hard to do. From the many hours of interviewing I had with her, I'd guess this is because her mother lived so irresponsibly for all the years Valerie was growing up. Except for the help she received from her grandparents, Valerie nearly raised herself. She did the chores around the house that were clearly her mother's to do. Not only did she take on the chores, she denied that she had done so. She didn't want to be removed from her home, so she got in the habit of protecting her mother. She was well aware of the power an authority might wield over the home situation.

Learning to be overly responsible has an upside, of course. It generally makes a person a great employee, a great neighbor, and a great friend, as long as too much responsibility doesn't take on the form of control. It also makes a person appreciative of others who do their share. But being overly responsible isn't what we should ever strive for. Instead, seeking a balanced view of how life should look, and then doing your part to make it so, is the goal. It's what leads to good relationships, happy families, comfortable work environments, and peaceful neighborhoods. Doing enough but not too much is the goal. And it's attainable.

Valerie has had to learn, with the help of the fellowship, how to let her mother and others take responsibility for themselves. Both sides of this equation—accepting our own responsibility and relinquishing others'—are so important to anyone wanting to function peacefully in their environment. And most of us in any kind of twelve-step program are seeking this kind of peace. If we stick around for "the miracle," as it's referred to, we will find it too. I have found it, but I know that maintaining it requires a continuing commitment to the suggestions the program offers.

I would say that Helene has found peace too. As was established when I shared aspects of her story earlier, she was a star when it came to acting out in her very dysfunctional family of origin. Being one of a dozen kids made acting out an understandable choice. But it also meant that she could easily slide under the radar screen. Too many to care for makes it difficult to care for any one child in the way he or she may need it. Her irresponsibility as a youth offers a great contrast to how very responsible she became, early in her recovery. Living in the program well affords the benefit of learning to be responsible when the circumstances call for it.

There is a fine line between being responsible and being overly responsible for the lives of others. It's an important line, however, and one that deserves constant adherence.

But there is much more than this to be said for Helene. One of the traits she has to fight against, even after many years on the recovery path, is not taking over the responsibilities of others. It's common to become overly responsible when you are the product of a dysfunctional family. Perhaps you are trying to make up for all the injury done to your family in the acting out stage. Or maybe it's simply a natural inclination when you discover how very freeing it is to be responsible for yourself. Whatever the case may be, Helene can be accused of caring too much about the behavior of others—for trying to change them when it really isn't her business to do so. There are worse things than caring too much, however. And Helene has a kind heart and a willingness to help. The universe can always use more of both.

Showing up in a responsible way in the lives of our friends, our families, and our colleagues is borne out of surviving an irresponsible family system. Responsibility is a trait, like the many others discussed throughout this book, that offers hope to any person who is still suffering in the bowels of the dysfunctional family. For sure we are affected by those childhood experiences, but we are not imprisoned for all time. There is a way out.

Before moving on to the final boost we can claim from surviving these families, let's review. We have had many examples of what responsibility looks like, how to attain it, and how to sustain it.

Offering to be helpful at the right moments, while not stepping in where others need to be in charge, is just one of the many responsible actions we can take.

Observing the many times others fail to take responsibility when they are clearly responsible offers us many helpful lessons.

It's not always easy to tell the difference between being controlling and taking a bit too much responsibility.

We can never force responsibility on to another person. We can only be willing to volunteer ourselves.

Doing for others what they must do themselves is never really appreciated. We do what we must do for ourselves.

Accepting responsibility where appropriate, and not taking it on where inappropriate, is evidence of good boundaries, good balance, and emotional maturity.

There is a fine line between being responsible and being overly responsible for the lives of others. It's an important line, however, and one that deserves constant adherence.

Further Reflection

Being responsible for ourselves in every respect—attitude, opinion, actions, and feelings—feels good. Respecting the demarcation separating us from others feels good too. Our desire to be kind can fool us into thinking we should do for others what is theirs to do. We need to be mindful every minute that personal responsibility is just that: personal.

13

Recognizing How Perfect Our Journey Has Been

We are coming into our own in the timing we need. For each of us it will be different, but for each of us, it will also be perfect.

Sonja Derian

It's with great joy that I say that my life has been divinely perfect. There were reasons for my many struggles, and the timing was perfect. The same can be claimed for my multiple successes. Wherever I was, whoever I was with, was heaven sent. Perhaps this sounds simplistic, but believing this gives me great comfort. I know I can count on my life unfolding in the same divine manner over the course of my remaining years.

I don't think I am the sole recipient of this perfect unfolding. The same holds true for us all. I'm convinced of it. We meet those people we need to meet. We teach those individuals who need what we can share. And we learn from the teachers who have lessons that are meant specifically for our ears. Like the scene in a beautiful tapestry, we each add a thread that must be present for the picture to be complete.

It soothes me to know that I myself sought out the many difficult experiences I have had in order to gain access to their underlying lesson. Additionally, it comforts me to know that my interactions, every single one of them, were necessary for my development and the development of contemporaries I met along the way. We were always in the right place at the right time, exchanging the right information. Hallelujah!

It makes all the difference in the world to feel certain of this as I look over my past and prepare for my future. The abuse I experienced as a young girl taught me forgiveness in a profound way. The abandonment issues that I stumbled over for decades allowed my mother and I to bond in an entirely unexpected, but truly special way, a way I couldn't have imagined and one that gave both of us freedom from the prison we had constructed. My fear of never measuring up pushed me to strive for goals that frightened me while also inspiring me. So much about my life escapes explanation, except to say that God was always doing for me what I couldn't have done by myself alone.

....

God is the motivator, the executor, and the way-shower.
We follow. We listen. We learn. Then we teach others.

....

Every person I interviewed had experiences that were unique in certain respects and yet similar to many of the threads in others' lives. One thing was certain: every person was on a path of experiences that stretched them in new directions while also affirming them in familiar ways that offered comfort. Being assured, as everyone eventually was, that whatever came their way was divinely intentional brought relief. Knowing that we are on God's radar screen keeps the wolves away.

It took some convincing to talk Marilyn into believing she had ever been on God's radar screen, however. The insanity in her home, evident in her dad's behavior, a man with a Ph.D. in psychiatry, had rocked her world to its core. "Why," was her awful and constant question. Of course, I had no sure answer, but suggested that her experiences in a household where mental illness dominated could help others to trust that they, too, could survive a home life that seemed bent on the destruction of every person in the family. Marilyn was living proof that survival was always possible, and even likely, if the awful family secrets were shared. In their very sharing, they became smaller, more manageable. And definitely survivable.

Marilyn's journey had many detours before she reached a destination that felt peaceful, but she never quit walking. She said she felt pulled to trust in each next step, again and again. Her constant refrain at the end of every sharing at a meeting was, "And I'll keep coming back." I was well aware that she understood, in a profound way, as did so many of us, that our own sanity, our own well-being, was tied to our commitment to show up, again and again. To show others that life, in the worst of times, could be made better.

We are strengthened every time we show others, by example, that nothing can destroy our resolve to survive but our own unwillingness.

I observed Marilyn leading by example, touching many who still tried to make sense of home situations that nearly matched the trauma and insanity that occurred behind her family's closed doors. Those of us who have survived and finally thrived as the result of living in a dysfunctional family understand, intuitively, how to help others move through the hidden land mines, even when they have come to feel almost normal. Marilyn's family was still as sick and troubled as it had been when she was a child. Nothing had really changed there. But *she* had changed. No longer was she held hostage by a dynamic that was intended to cripple her and her siblings, as well as her mother. Her sense of humor, her perseverance, and her ability to detach but not shun were remarkable and highly developed traits. And perhaps most of all, she had embraced kindness without having been shown very much of it in her family of origin.

Marilyn's experiences, in so many regards, matched those of a number of my interviewees, who shared so many of her strengths in spades. I'd like to focus on Janet again because she took people under her wing much like Marilyn did. She was able to do this because she kept no secrets—everyone was allowed to know her story fully, and thus she frequently drew the neediest people seeking help. They could see in her an honesty, a grateful willingness to forgive the awfulness of the past, and a freedom from judgment that was attractive and sought by many.

We begin to see that those loving qualities that are missing in our homes can be sought and found and embraced in other settings. Healing can begin anywhere.

In case you have forgotten, Janet, like Marilyn, was abused but not by a dad. Rather it was an older brother, an act he admitted to and her parents denied in spite of his confession, making the insanity of the household even harder to grapple with. Janet was able to forgive her brother because he said he was sorry, but she struggled to forgive her parents. Their insistence that her experiences were made up made her feel unimportant, unloved, and unvalued. It took a herculean effort for her to learn to love and value herself, but she got there, and only because she was surrounded by people in the rooms who expressed unconditional love, day in and day out. Their love finally permeated her walls.

Unfortunately, while still trying to recover from her family of origin's denial of her experiences, Janet married a man who was narcissistic as well as paranoid, and the recovery she was gradually claiming in regard to her family was nearly wiped out by the experiences she had with her husband. Every behavior she was devoted to developing, in the hopes of perfecting it in time, was put to the test. Again and again. He was sick to the core. And he tried to make her sick too. Fortunately, she was bound and determined to keep moving forward, and with the encouragement of her many friends, she got the courage to leave him.

Our strengths seem to multiply when we exercise them, one by one.

It wasn't easy to escape. In fact it was harrowing at times. He stalked her and she chose to carry a non-lethal weapon. He pleaded; she changed the door locks. He followed her; she got a different car. He moved into her neighborhood. She changed every route she drove. Throughout the entire time, she held him up to the light, praying that he would find peace. He was not going to hold her hostage, ever again. Of this she was sure. Because she had learned so much in the rooms, she was able to free him from her judgment, and take responsibility for her actions, not his.

When it came to detachment, perhaps the most freeing of all the gifts we ultimately get when we let go of our dysfunctional family of origin, Janet had more work to do. That's one of the qualities we all have to practice, each day anew. If we could do it once, for all time, we'd not seek the support we keep going to meetings to get. It's my supposition that that's how it's meant to be. We are needed in the fellowship. For all time—not just until we get a little bit better. We are needed there for all of the folks who show up after our arrival. What a sad world this would be if the rooms were empty.

Janet learned from watching, and she got a mentor who listened, another quality we hone as the result of never being heard in our unhealthy families. Her "teacher" said, over and over, let go of him, his memory, his behavior, his past, and yours too. His presence in your life taught you all you ever needed to learn. He was there for a reason but that chapter is now closed. Janet glommed on to that explanation and inched forward. Baby steps at first. Detachment was freedom. She knew that. She also could see that her work was unending for the time being. Her friends surrounded her and practiced with her the very same traits she was trying to master. Both the imitation and the modeling of these traits for one another made living all that much easier.

....

The perfection in our journey cannot be seen except with hindsight.

....

Janet served as a great role model for many. As I related before, one of her favorite phrases, offered on behalf of anyone who troubled her, was "Bless his heart." And she meant it. It changed her mindset in the moment and always left a lingering good feeling with others. I know that I, for one, always experienced a shift in my perception when I heard it. Janet didn't say it in a flip way. She meant it. She firmly believed that we are all capable of getting off track, and getting a nudge from the God of one's understanding can always help us change direction.

I watched a number of our mutual friends and colleagues have a change of heart when Janet was around. We all know how the bad moods of others can interfere with our good moods, if we aren't careful; the same can be true of good moods. Someone's positive mood can rub off. And in this way, Janet helped many. The overall change from who she had been because of her unhealthy family and unhealthy marriage, to who she was becoming, was a sharp contrast and one that fortunately showed others how absolutely possible change was. It began with a decision and was followed by action. Then practice made the change take hold.

No bad experience in our life has to be the only experience that forms who we are for all time.

One of the people who practiced new behavior with a vengeance was Sheri. Dysfunction never looked more devastating; her story ranked among the toughest of all. In every arm of the family going back many generations, alcoholism and many other forms of dysfunction caused nearly total destruction. And that's not the worst part of it. There was not a single person in her family tree who *ever* sought help! Because she was lucky enough to have a counselor suggest Al-Anon because of her troubled marriage, Sheri got a new lease on life. She got to break the family pattern. She wasn't able to change any one else, of course, but she changed herself.

No one else has to change for us to get a new lease on our "perfect" life.

Sheri was a role model like none other. She understood detachment in such a clear way. She lived it. And others could see it in her actions. She demonstrated kindness by never taking umbrage at what another person might say or do. She excused their acts of unkindness as owing to fear or ignorance. (Even if they might have meant them that way.) She was the embodiment of surrender. And to the pleasure of all who knew her, she never failed to listen lovingly and intently to your every word. None of these qualities had been hers before entering the fellowship, she said. She was as bent on vengeance as the next wounded soul. But she was patient, a good student, and a willing modeler of the new behaviors that carried her old self away.

Sheri embodied resilience—her journey was not easy. Even after years in the fellowship, she was faced with a level of dissension in her family that could well have destroyed another person. She simply walked through or around the dissension and moved on. As I already said, she understood detachment to a tee. And her demonstration of it, along with her explanation of it, made her a truly sought after teacher and mentor. I watched her from afar on many occasions as she approached people who were hurting, offering to be a guide, a friend, a sponsor. She never let anyone walk away unaided if she could offer a helping hand. And she never doubted that her past was perfect, making her present perfect too.

Sheri didn't possess any of these traits when she came to the fellowship. None of them. But she had an uncanny understanding *that she had been sent in order to bring others along.* She knew it and I knew it too as soon as we sat down to talk. Her very presence in my life confirmed what I had already come to believe: *there are no accidents. We meet who we need to meet. We learn what we need to learn and we teach what we need to teach to those who have been divinely selected to be our students.* Praise be to God!

....

Everyone has a plan that is already unfolding. If they are heading toward you, be ready. You need them.

....

Sheri taught each one of us the value of trusting in the process. She showed each one of us how to live with faith. And she practiced her many lessons for all of us to see and grow from. That's the payoff from being in the rooms of the fellowship with others who, like you, are trying to escape the destruction of a family that is haunted by or still living in the midst of dysfunction, as Sheri's was. For her, this was life or death. We cheered her efforts to make every day a good one, for her and for us.

I haven't referred to Dawn for a while but the success of her journey deserves our attention. Like Sheri and Valerie, Dawn's family of origin was so devastated by the disease of alcoholism (and many other ism's and abuses too), that I doubt I myself could have survived if we had traded homes as children. She was resilient even before she knew what that word meant. She was able to laugh and had an extremely wry sense of humor. Her heart was huge and full of love for anyone who needed it. And she had to practice acceptance from morning until night because of all the turmoil and disease in her family, her friends, and her community, the reservation.

Dawn kept her nose to the grindstone. She had been taught to believe that her creator was always waiting to serve her needs, and she wanted to trust that. Even though she had felt abandoned as a child, she knew he had always been there. She simply couldn't always feel His presence. When we first talked, she was struggling to believe that her journey, in every aspect, was divinely charted. It's hard for any of us to understand that the experience of sexual and physical abuse could be in any way valuable in childhood, but we have to come to terms with it if we want to know peace. I explain it this way, to myself and others: it's not that the abuse itself is valuable, but rather that through it we are given a valuable chance to learn about the human condition and then teach others in the decades following. I have to take it on faith that my experiences as a child were useful because I have been able to share them with other women, sharing, in particular, the good stuff about forgiveness that I might not have learned in such a profound way from any other experience.

I very simply believe that every step of my journey was perfect. I believe the same is true of Dawn's. Of Sheri's. Of Janet's and Valerie's too. In fact, there is not a man or woman I spoke with who didn't have the journey that was right for them. My heart knows this. My mind believes this. And I'm grateful to have come to this place of acceptance.

We have met by design. You have met everyone on your path by design as well. Your journey into tomorrow is part of your truth. Believe this, and peace will be yours.

In closing this chapter, I'd like to briefly turn to Allison once again. She told me she was certain that her struggle in her family of origin, including their alcoholism, was the preparation she needed to face and then survive the devastating cancer she got at a time when her marriage was rocky and her children were small. She knew that since she had survived her family and her disease, she had the strength to survive the cancer diagnosis too. Her crippled body, even today, is her badge of survival. It didn't destroy her. It made her stronger. It allows all of us to see that the worst that befalls us can be used as a stepping stool to more growth, more faith, more acceptance.

We came here not knowing what for. We learn why while we are here. What better information can there be?

Before moving into the final chapter of concluding thoughts, let's review what this chapter drove home:

God is the motivator, the executor, the way-shower. We follow. We listen. We learn. Then we teach others.

We are strengthened every time we show others, by example, that nothing can destroy our resolve to survive but our unwillingness.

We begin to see that those loving qualities that are missing in our homes can be sought and found and embraced in other settings. Healing can begin anywhere.

Our strengths seem to multiply when we exercise them, one by one.

The perfection in our journey cannot be seen except with hindsight. We can, however, choose to believe it while it's taking place.

No bad experience in our life has to be the only experience that forms who we are for all time.

No one else has to change for us to get a new lease on our "perfect" life.

Everyone has a plan that is already unfolding. If they are heading toward you, be ready. You need them.

We have met by design. You have met everyone on your path by design as well. Your journey into tomorrow is part of your truth. Believe this and peace will be yours.

Further Reflection

Accepting that we are reading this because it's part of our necessary assignment brings comfort, I hope. I am comforted by believing it has been my assignment to write it.

14

Going On, Going in Peace

In three words I can sum up everything I've learned about life: it goes on.

Robert Frost

I am so grateful to have been accompanied on my search for "the good stuff" by more than two dozen survivors of families rife with dysfunction. These survivors not only willingly shared their stories, but in exploring them realized that they had thrived as a result of their experiences. That was a big deal to them and to me. I don't think any of us expected to discover what we were looking for with such power and clarity. The good stuff is really there.

No one wants to grow up in a dysfunctional system. We didn't even have that name for it as youngsters, but it is what we got, and how fortunate it is that good can come from living in even the most troubling, threatening circumstances. In fact, I can say that a person may never know just how creative and capable they are until they are confronted by a situation that has the capacity to overwhelm them in the blink of an eye.

I was amazed by every one of the people I interviewed. And I am floored by their knowledge, courage, and continuing level of engagement in not only their own healing and growth, but in others' as well. No one voiced that they felt intentionally exploited or in grave danger because of their parenting, or lack thereof. No one felt it necessary to divorce his or her family after leaving home. Some needed space, on occasion, and still do, and that's a healthy choice when the family dynamics become too toxic. But each person, and I include myself in this group, came to believe that repairing, even strengthening, all those familial relationships was beneficial—personally, and for the family as a whole.

I would even venture to say that this healing benefits the entire human community, even if we aren't consciously aware of helping the rest of humankind. This universal effect on others, as noted earlier in the book, can be attributed to "the butterfly effect."

The butterfly effect is evident everywhere, all of the time. It does not need to be seen or even believed for it to make its mark.

This effect envelops all of us, whether we are conscious of it or not. *A butterfly, gently moving his wings around the flowers on my deck, is ever so gently affecting my neighbor's flowers too, as well as the breeze moving through town, and the storm that will be created next week. What an awesome occurrence.*

Additionally, according to Heisenberg's uncertainty principle, which dates back to 1927, the specific involvement of any one of us necessarily also influences however the effect evolves, creating yet another layer of impact. I think the good news here is that science assures us that each individual positive action has a broader effect than it might have been intended to have initially. For example, when we put our differences aside or forgive members of our family of origin, we are actually affecting our relationships with many others too. And that's of great benefit to the human community.

What good food for thought. Whatever you or I do or say gets paid forward, giving each of us a valuable opportunity to effect real, positive change in the world we inhabit. Unfortunately, (and this is very unfortunate indeed), everyone's bad actions have their impact too, making it all the more necessary that those of us who want to create a loving universe should go to great lengths to act positively, over and over again.

When I consider my own family of origin and the way we influenced one another, I'm amazed. I embrace the idea that we *chose each other*. We sought one another out for what we would teach and learn in our time together.

Little by little, I could see that it wasn't just my family—I was sharing a mission with every person I was involved with. And the same was true for the people I interviewed. We seldom see this early in our relationships, but it's there, and if we are open to it, we can feel it. And then it comforts us. Really comforts us.

We are where we need to be and with whom we need to share that space, every moment. No exceptions.

Whether interviewing William, Marilee, Helene, Allison, Dawn, or Celia, I was occasionally moved to tears by the stories they shared. When I think of Carl, and how damaged his psyche was at the hands of a fearful, angry father, I am deeply moved that he not only survived, but eventually thrived in ways that influenced his own children so positively. The same is true about all of the people I interviewed. No one was completely diminished. Everyone eventually, with the help of some other loving companion, coupled with the God of their understanding, managed to create a comfortable life for themselves. I stand in awe of all of them. Let's do a final review now. Let's look at these individual traits again, and how they manifested in a few of the interviewees. This will serve as fodder for growth, I hope, for anyone who thinks life is simply too hard because of the family he or she was dealt.

First there is resilience . . .

Resilience. Why is it so important? I believe its importance lies in the fact that it represents to others who are looking on that in spite of criticism, even unrelenting and undeserved punishment, we can get up again and again and move forward, not unscathed but not defeated completely.

Resilience means toughness. Undefeated in spite of difficulties. Being able to stand tall even though the attacks are unrelenting.

Even though Carl's father was unrelenting in his humiliation and criticism, Carl survived and eventually became a very different kind of father to his own children. His inner strength allowed him to thrive in ways that were beyond the reach of his own father. Carl knew the power of love, what he gave and what he received. And that power groomed him to become a man of great character—one who understood the value of praise.

Resilience is a necessary quality in the life of any successful person, I think. It may show up in myriad ways, but it often manifests in the ability to recover quickly from an attack, whether it's intentional or accidental. To be resilient also means *not letting failure deter you from the willingness to try again.* Dawn was beaten down again and again, physically as well as psychologically. But she is standing tall today. Nearly forty years after her journey into the rooms of recovery began, she is meeting each day with determination, letting the many past traumas live in the past. She knows they have no place in a sane, secure present. As I said in the first chapter, "there is nothing magical about resilience. It's a decision before it's anything else. And then it's a commitment to execute the plan."

Perseverance is next . . .

Along with resilience, **perseverance** is a quality I observed in the many I interviewed. I'm grateful it's one of the qualities I developed too. In fact, it's the quality that positioned me to write a dissertation when I had no real plan for where I was going and had not previously even voiced a desire for a doctorate. With nowhere else to go, I simply began heading in that direction after my first marriage ended. After years of study, after all the course work and written exams were completed, I dutifully sat from 8 AM until noon every day and read and wrote. Three hundred pages later I was done, and a Ph.D. was my payoff. Truth be told, I was as surprised as any one of my friends. Perseverance was the key.

Willingness is the first necessary step to the successful completion of any task or goal.

Not a single interviewee lacked perseverance. They didn't all share this quality equally, of course, but it did become clear that this is one of the necessary traits of any person who wants to survive the dysfunctional family system. I wrote about William's commitment to being academically successful and a good athlete. He was determined to find his place in society since he felt no security living at home with either parent.

Valerie demonstrated it too, as you will recall. She was steadfast in her search to succeed even though her childhood was a living hell. She quite simply did not give up, even when she wanted to. Janet, Charlie, and Allison also score high in terms of perseverance. They didn't let the occasional failures block their commitment to trying again. And again. One might even say, in Charlie's case, that failure to get that first job as a pilot inspired him to try even harder. He knew a job was there. He simply didn't know where there was.

Switching gears somewhat, let's look now at laughter . . .

I think it's fortunate that a sense of humor can be cultivated. In the dysfunctional family, laughter is often a scarce commodity, except when it's disparaging. But each person I spoke with for this book laughed often and heartily, and said that being able to see the humor in situations, both those that were funny and some that were serious, had saved them multiple times. Charlie again comes to mind. Being the practical joker in his family was a well-honed trait, but it wasn't lost on him that he clung to it because it also served as an effective wall between him and others. Knowing how to be funny was helpful in those many instances when he needed to soften the sharp edges of the humorous jabs he took at others.

Laughing over the genuinely funny occurrences in one's life, as well as the more serious ones, equalizes all the circumstances. And that's a good thing.

It was easy to see that hindsight helped cast a far more favorable perspective on so many formerly troubling situations with all of the people I interviewed. It was also apparent that every person I talked to wanted to take life less seriously than they had lived it before. They clearly felt the value of this through the visceral impact of a good laugh.

Laughing moves the soul. Making the choice to revisit some experiences that we can see now were actually pretty funny is a great way to change our perspective on life, past and present. Some people joke that it's never too late to have a happy childhood.

Now let's revisit forgiveness, to some the most valuable of all the tools we learn to appreciate and use.

Within all the families I was privy to through my interviews, it was easy to see the need for forgiveness. No one had been unscathed in their upbringing. Everyone had been abused in some manner: emotionally or physically or mentally. Some, like Janet and Dawn, had even suffered the grave injustice of sexual abuse. Each person, regardless of the kind or level of abuse, had come to understand that they needed to forgive their perpetrators if they were to find any peace of mind in the present.

There is certainly no intention here to excuse the abuse. But I do want to stress that if a person doesn't let it go, finally, he or she will tread water, staying stuck in old perceptions rather than opening the door to new awareness. We live to grow, and there simply isn't any growth if we wallow in the past, letting it hurt us over and over again.

Forgiveness isn't as hard as one might imagine. It's a decision, and once made, the steps for moving forward are laid out for us. Additionally, one's Higher Power generally ushers toward us the very individuals we need to forgive. But let's remember too, forgiving *ourselves* is part of the equation. And for what? For our own faults, as well as the many judgments we harbor against others, which contributes to our "stuckness."

Forgiveness is surely a gift that shifts the entire human community.

Forgiveness had made each of my interviewees more vulnerable, gentle, open to expressing love, and intentional about helping others. Forgiveness closes the separation between all of us. It melts the barriers our egos want to maintain, but can't when we let others really know us. Forgiveness is an act of love. Even Carl, who was harmed so mercilessly, sang the praises of forgiveness. He knew it had changed him for the better. He knew it had made the relationships he had with his wife and his children more solid, more loving, more authentic.

One of my observations was that forgiveness seemed to be the act that contributed most to healing the aching heart. Why that's true wasn't easy to determine, at first, but after many conversations I was able to see that my interviewees' lives simply shifted when they let others off the hook. One courageous act after another changes the world we inhabit. The sweet irony is that hurt people can lessen the hurt in the world, if they make the choice to do so. We have all heard the saying, "hurt people hurt people." But that's not how it has to be.

It's time to move on, and surrendering comes next . . .

Controlling anyone who is bugging us for any reason is simply out of the question. We may think we have legitimate reasons for taking control, and when it's a youngster or a teenager in our home, perhaps we should be allowed to take control, but it doesn't work. It simply doesn't work. Taking charge of someone else's behavior or opinion may seem like a reasonable task—it may even seem like a reasonable solution to any number of problems as we have outlined them—but *exactly no one* can be forced against his or her will to do what is requested or even demanded. Getting comfortable with the idea of surrendering others to their own choices, behavior, opinions, or even ideas is the far easier path to take. Every person I interviewed finally had to grow comfortable with this path.

....

Surrendering allows our fellow travelers to be whomever they choose to be.

....

Only once we accept the initial shock of having no control over others, can we appreciate the notion of surrender. I'm thinking right now of Harry. If you will recall, Harry went into business with a man he had known for some time who he considered reputable. They opened a restaurant and within two years, much to Harry's shock, they had gone bankrupt.

What Harry was unaware of was the dishonesty of his partner—dishonesty so deep that he managed to steal and squander all the business' bank receipts without Harry knowing it. Following the discovery, no matter how hard Harry tried to get his partner to confess his behavior and do what was necessary to file for bankruptcy, his partner refused to budge. In fact, he disappeared. It fell on Harry's shoulders to be accountable for the entire failure of the business.

Even when our viewpoint appears right and justifiable, as in Harry's case, we still can't make someone else do what they don't want to do. Period! Every person I spoke with had struggled against the idea of giving up control. "If I say it this way, perhaps . . ." or "If I agree to do this, then he will do that," and on and on. We finally have to say, "I give. You have the final say about your life." And then the relief sets in.

Surrendering actually releases tension. It changes how every circumstance feels. The freedom gained through surrender registers universally.

No other practice offers such immediate freedom. It's a freedom we are not eager to relinquish once we have tasted it. And surrendering, in time, will be recognized as the biggest gift given to the human community.

And then there is connection . . .

Our connection to others and the healing it offers can't be weighed too heavily. It has been said that it's in joining with others that we heal. The isolation of disconnection holds us back, keeps us stuck and sick and desperately lonely.

Connecting with others isn't easy for many of us, unfortunately. The men and women I interviewed all dreaded going to their first counselor or support group or recovery room. Keeping the dysfunction of the family to themselves seemed safer. It was a common hope that maybe they had even imagined it. The ugliness of the dysfunction made them too afraid to let others in on how their families actually looked on the inside. But everyone I spoke with had finally surrendered to their inner cry for help. That's where our paths crossed.

I'm so grateful to each one of them because of what I learned, but also because I firmly believe that every time we share our pain, we lessen it. And every time we share our joy, we double it. In this book, more pain has been shared than joy perhaps, but every person here has crossed the bridge to a better life filled with joy. No one more than Marilyn. You will recall that her father was a psychiatrist who threatened everyone in the family, especially her mother, with beatings if they let others know what life at home was really like. In the next breath he'd deny that his words were ever spoken.

Not feeling crazy in that home was impossible. That Marilyn had the courage, and I do mean courage, to escape and get help for herself was fortunate for all of us who knew her and loved her. She taught us memorable things about the value of connection and the path to joy. She was a living example of how it had saved her life.

....

Vulnerably connecting with others absolutely heals our ailing souls.

....

The added benefit of learning to connect with others as we do in recovery rooms, as all the people I have shared with you here have learned to do, is that it closes the separation between us, a separation that has the capacity to destroy the human spirit. Without conscious connection we die. We simply die.

Love is the answer to any situation, any question, any person . . .

We are acting from a place of either love or fear in every instance of our life. Simplistic? Perhaps, but true. Sheri taught me so much about this idea. Rather, I should say showed me so much. She was the embodiment of love. Her teaching about love was constant and it offered hope and help to those who walked through the doors of recovery rooms. She was love in action.

Sheri had not grown up in a home where love was practiced, however. She learned about love from others in the rooms who mentored her, and then she took her turn. That's how healing happens. Love is passed on to the uninitiated when it is least expected. Wounds are closed and the messages of hope and love are received and not squandered. They will be passed on again and again when someone else seeks a new way to see, to understand, without even knowing what they are looking for.

I didn't end up in my first twelve-step room in search of what I received. But I was hooked from the start. And why? The feeling of love that permeated the space, the faces, the laughter of those who were present. I wanted what they had. I went back to get more of it.

We can't help but recognize love when we see it so freely expressed.

My life has never been the same since that first encounter with real love in 1974. I know the same can safely be said for all the people I have shared with you throughout the pages of this book. We came. We sought. We found. We shared. We healed.

Putting our differences aside when we love each other benefits the world too.

Love is a constant. We learn to recognize it in others before we can see it in ourselves.

Kindness begins here and now with one simple decision . . .

When others are not kind, they are hurting. I have chosen to believe this idea, true or not, and it has changed my life. Marilee is one of the women I interviewed who reflected this philosophy in every word she said and every action she took. Like so many others, she didn't grow up in an environment that taught her about kindness, but she did observe how it was expressed by others. She then became a strong proponent.

Being kind is a choice that can be repeated as many times a day as necessary.

Barriers melted away, Marilee said, when she began offering the hand of kindness to others. Nettie was quick to agree with her. I talked with both of them about this topic of dysfunctional families and how they had been affected. It was enlightening to get their views—two women from very different backgrounds and sections of the country. One a professional all her life, the other a housewife. One with an alcoholic husband who never quit drinking, the other with siblings who would rather drink than interact with her. But both of them sang the praises of the expression of kindness, what it did in the moment, and how it benefitted the rest of the day too.

It's not lost on me that what we do to one, we do to all. What we carry in our hearts has its impact too. We need not even be aware of this for it to be true. William comes to mind in relation to kindness. Even though he experienced none in his home while growing up, I would have to say he was one of the nicest men I had the pleasure of talking to. How did the transformation happen? By osmosis, I think.

William came into the rooms to find out how to help his wife, you might recall. Much like all of us who have similar problems, he thought he would be handed a small booklet outlining what to do to change how she behaved. That was what I was seeking, too. I think that's what we all seek initially. He got help, but not that kind. And he observed the power of kindness. Kindness that he got from others, "for doing nothing," he said, and the kindness he heard others talk about: its power, its effect on the family, its ability to change any circumstance at all.

Don't be stingy with kindness. Offer it to everyone.

It is always good to check our motives regarding any behavior. Kindness as an attempt to influence others through manipulation is not healthy behavior. But I have decided that choosing to be kind is always a good and wise choice because of its far-reaching benefit throughout the human community. And the way in which it subtly changes the one being kind too.

And now, detachment, a powerful game changer . . .

I didn't understand what detachment meant when I first heard the word. I didn't even have an inkling. My life consisted of a series of attachments to people, particularly men. Not living that way seemed impossible, uninteresting, certainly lonely. I honestly didn't know if it was possible to detach my mind, my emotions, and my behavior from the actions of the person I was dancing around. I certainly had not gone to a twelve-step meeting to learn how to do this. On the contrary, I wanted to learn how to make every hostage I hung on to want to stay. Codependency, they called it. Another term unfamiliar to me.

Detaching from others lets them and us live as we all should live.

The individuals I interviewed all had attachment problems too. I'd venture to say it's a common syndrome in the human community, and not just here in America. Wars are fought over the misunderstood actions and reactions of people living across borders from one another, or even more commonly, living halfway around the world from one another. Is it any wonder that minding our own business and celebrating each other's individual journey is difficult?

I can point to any one of the interviewees and elaborate on how the failure to detach from a lover, a child, a sibling, or a parent prevented them from living peacefully, but my own story serves well too. My life was a series of unhealthy attachments, coupled with the complications and dark drama that one expects when alcohol and drugs are part of the mix. I loved my "hostages," and the thought of being uncoupled from them—detached from them, as was suggested in Al-Anon—simply scared me too much. Who would I be without them? How would I live if someone wasn't in my constant sight?

Discovering that I had never had a real life at all was such an unexpected gift. Every person I spoke with received this gift too, and what's even better is that we became strong proponents for letting go of the others we felt needed us, when in reality, we thought we'd die without them.

....

We will find no peace of mind until we free others to live their own lives.

....

To listen is to witness. No greater gift can we offer . . .

Listening to our fellow travelers may be the best gift we can offer. I certainly had the experience of feeling unheard for much of my life. It smacks of the too-familiar adage from an earlier generation, that children should be "seen and not heard." It's my observation that unfortunately this trait hasn't died out in dysfunctional families. Those I interviewed concurred.

Feeling discounted or judged in an uncomplimentary way are common themes in dysfunctional families. One idea I discovered, which lay at the root of all dysfunctional families, was that only one person really counted and that was the person who had usurped the power from everyone else.

....

Being heard is for many the first step on the path to healing.

....

We give ourselves a gentle gift by looking to the folks in recovery circles as the parents we may never have had. I have yet to meet someone in any twelve-step program, or in any part of my journey, who didn't need some re-parenting. And it's not my intention to put parents down here. I think we can only give others what we were given. And no doubt few were raised with really healthy parenting. The beauty of twelve-step groups is that we listen. We care. We share. We make ourselves humble before one another and we admit our failings. All of this educates the newcomers and reeducates the old timers about our purpose, and it's a simple one: listen and love. Accept and honor. Whatever we failed to get at home can be made up for here, in this setting.

No one I spoke with manifested this more clearly than Marilee. Whether in the circle at a meeting or one to one, she never looked away when a person was speaking. You knew she heard you. You knew she cared. You knew that if you were sharing a hurt, it was being halved at that very moment. She wasn't the only person with this trait, but she generally went one step further than others. After listening, at the end of a meeting or over coffee, she approached you with a genuine hug, and that hug sealed the deal. You were on your way to real healing.

This gift of Marilee's was honed, even though her family never gave her what she was able to give to others. How is this possible, I used to wonder? And then other aspects of my spiritual journey answered the question. We each are here with an assignment. We get the parents and the families we need in order to grow into the people we need to become. Marilee did it before our eyes. So did Sheri. So did everyone I spoke with. The equation is actually pretty simple when we look at it this way, isn't it? We become who we need to be. We meet who we need to meet. We teach and learn what is assigned to us. And listening is one of those lessons.

I think it's an interesting conundrum that what we didn't get from our families growing up, we do find where we'd least expect it: in a room of strangers who also have been deeply wounded by their upbringing.

Judgment traps while acceptance releases. Choose . . .

Judgment, when it is negative, is never helpful. That's primarily because it's used to criticize others. Discernment, on the other hand, which is akin to judgment, is considered helpful because it determines value. We choose, again and again, to judge or discern. Most parenting in dysfunctional families ranks high on negative judgment. And we gravitate to mimicking whatever we observed at home. But we can learn to "discern" with kinder, clearer eyes. And when we do, we discover the power and the joy of acceptance.

Acceptance is the solution that changes the tenor of every stress-filled moment.

William and Carl lived in a storm of negative judgment until they finally escaped from the clutches of one or both parents. And yet, they excelled in their own lives in many ways. One was their willingness to lay negative judgments aside and practice love and acceptance freely. They did for their children what they wished could have been done for them. In the process, they re-parented themselves and became great examples to everyone, reminding us that acceptance is attainable.

We can sit in judgment of those who trouble us all we want, but nothing changes if nothing changes. If we want to experience something different in our families, among our friends, at work, or in our neighborhoods, we must pick up the reins of change ourselves. It became apparent to me (and to all the people I interviewed and observed) that the easiest solution was changing our *own* minds, choosing a different approach ourselves, and accepting others as they were and are. There is relief in this reality, actually, and it's this: we can be assured that change will occur if we are in the driver's seat, responsible for acceptance.

Acceptance, unfortunately, isn't a natural response. It requires a decision, then commitment, and lots of practice.

Every person who was part of the small research project for this book practiced day in and day out. And they knew the old behavior was still trying to reclaim them. All our old behaviors sit in the shadows and wait for those vulnerable moments to reassert themselves. Being our better self in all of our affairs requires vigilance.

Accepting responsibility for our own lives is the first step to true healing . . .

We take a big step in our healing when we give up the desire to blame others for whatever befalls us. However, we have to give up the desire to control others too. Responsibility for others' actions is not part of our job description. Others cross our path for many reasons, but that is never one of them. In order to embrace emotional maturity, we must respect others enough to let them be responsible for themselves and respect ourselves enough to take responsibility for every part of our own lives.

Responsibility goes both ways, and is a necessary hallmark of one who wants true healing.

···

Not stepping in to take charge, when it's not ours to take, shows real growth.

···

This is one trait that demands willingness for everyone to attain, I think. When we blame others, or are slow to accept full responsibility for screw-ups, we often chalk it up to human nature. Wanting to share the blame feels easier than saying, "it's my fault that this happened." I think that's what makes responsibility such a high priority for the many people I interviewed. They had all survived such high levels of dysfunction that it wouldn't have been surprising if they had wanted to push responsibility for mistakes on to others. They surely didn't observe parents taking responsibility for lousy parenting. And yet, these folks demonstrated they had turned the corner, and supported each other in turning that same corner.

Every person I interviewed wore responsibility very well. Some of them struggled not to take on someone else's, on occasion, but blamers they weren't. And that's refreshing.

···

Being controlling can look like being responsible, if we aren't careful. And honest with ourselves. However, there is a big difference between the two.

···

Patty, perhaps, wore this "achievement" the best of all the people I spoke with. She had a sixth sense when it came to responsibility versus control. She knew what was hers to do, even before she got to the rooms of recovery.

But among us she learned what *not* to do. She didn't answer phones that didn't need to be answered. She didn't ask or answer questions that were none of her business. She didn't blame, in spite of the upbringing she had. She seemed to understand that her parents had done their best with her big family. What they did wasn't great, but it was past. Today was her day. A new day. And she could make choices that benefitted her and her children.

Patty was a great role model, especially for the newcomers to our rooms of recovery. She had a great sense of humor and had survived many ordeals. She took them in stride, and this demonstrated to everyone that responsibility begins with "us." Responsibility leads to manageability. And Patty managed very well.

The journey has been perfect . . .

Coming to the conclusion that our journey has been exactly what we needed offers great relief. I'm personally overjoyed that I have been called to do the work I do, and that it has allowed me to meet and interview each person who has been part of this book. And when I look back on my life, from my childhood to the present, I can see clearly how every *thread of my tapestry* was necessary. Every corner I turned, whether into a dark alley or down an unfamiliar street, introduced me to experiences I needed to be the woman writing this book at this very moment.

I know this is true for Carl and William and Janet. In fact, every kind person who gave me their time, their honesty, their attention, and their willingness to share the details of harrowing pasts is to be commended. Every one of them is on a path that offers hope to others. I thank each and every person who sat with me, and in so doing became part of my evolution, part of my tapestry as I became part of theirs. We needed each other. As I said so much earlier in the book, the decision to make this a part of our journey was decided long before we ever met. What a glorious awareness that has become for me. It makes every new day rich with anticipation.

....

We have met by design. Thank you for showing up.

....

In closing, let me leave you with a reiteration of a few simple, life-altering ideas. I know my life has never been the same since adopting these ideas.

The butterfly effect is evident everywhere, all the time. It does not need to be seen or even believed for it to make its mark.

We are where we need to be and with whom we need to share that space, every moment. No exceptions.

Resilience means toughness. Undefeated in spite of difficulties. Being able to stand tall even though the attacks are unrelenting.

Willingness is the first necessary step to successful completion of any task or goal.

Laughing over the genuinely funny occurrences in one's life, as well as the more serious ones, makes all circumstances equal in their overall impact. And that's a good thing.

Forgiveness is a gift that shifts the entire human community.

Surrendering allows our fellow travelers to be whoever they choose to be.

Surrendering actually releases tension. It changes how every circumstance feels.

Vulnerably connecting with others is the only thing that can absolutely heal our ailing souls.

We can't help but recognize love when we see it so freely expressed.

Putting our differences aside when we love each other benefits the world too.

Being kind is a choice that can be repeated as many times a day as necessary.

Don't be stingy with kindness. Offer it to everyone.

Detaching from others lets them (and us) live as we all should live.

We will find no peace of mind until we free others to live their own lives.

Being heard is for many the first step on the path to healing.

Listening is an art that needs constant practice. And it creates its own payoff: intimacy.

Acceptance is the solution that changes the tenor of every stress-filled moment.

Acceptance, unfortunately, isn't a natural response. It requires a decision, then commitment, and lots of practice.

Not stepping in to take charge unless it's ours to take shows real growth.

Being controlling can look like being responsible if we aren't careful.

We have met by design. Our work here is by design. Our legacy has been determined. Hallelujah.

....

Go in peace and know that your journey is divine.

....

ABOUT THE AUTHOR

PHOTO CREDIT: JOE CASEY

Karen Casey is a writer and workshop facilitator for 12-step recovery. She is the author of 26 books about addiction and recovery, among them *Each Day a New Beginning, Change Your Mind and Your Life Will Follow, Codependence and the Power of Detachment.* She lectures across the United States, Canada, Mexico, Germany, Spain, and Ireland, carrying her message of hope for others on the road to recovery.

TO OUR READERS

Conari Press, an imprint of Red Wheel/Weiser, publishes books on topics ranging from spirituality, personal growth, and relationships to women's issues, parenting, and social issues. Our mission is to publish quality books that will make a difference in people's lives—how we feel about ourselves and how we relate to one another. We value integrity, compassion, and receptivity, both in the books we publish and in the way we do business.

Our readers are our most important resource, and we appreciate your input, suggestions, and ideas about what you would like to see published.

Visit our website at *www.redwheelweiser.com* to learn about our upcoming books and free downloads, and be sure to go to *www.redwheelweiser.com/newsletter* to sign up for newsletters and exclusive offers.

You can also contact us at *info@rwwbooks.com*.

Conari Press
an imprint of Red Wheel/Weiser, LLC
665 Third Street, Suite 400
San Francisco, CA 94107

403

235

2005

Beg 1

6304

Burbank

Rd SE